THE WORLD ENCYCLOPEDIA OF

MOTORCYCLES

THE WORLD ENCYCLOPEDIA OF
MOTORCYCLES

A COMPLETE MARQUE-BY-MARQUE ENCYCLOPEDIA

Roland Brown

HH

HERMES
HOUSE

🏍 ACKNOWLEDGEMENTS

The publishers would like to thank the following for their kind permission to reproduce their photographs:

Martyn Barnwell/EMAP and EMAP Archives 7, 8, 14t/b, 30t/b, 32t, 40 (all), 41b, 48b, 57ml/mr, 67bl, 68t, 69t, 70 (all), 103tr, 106t, 108m, 115t, 121m, 124, 125tl, 126 (all), 127tl/ml, 128 (all), 129 (all), 122ml, 124t, 130t, 132t, 142m, 151tmr/br, 152t, 153t/r 3 down. **Roland Brown** Front flap, 10t, 11b, 23t, 25tl/br/bl, 35tl, 37bl, 43b, 44b, 46m/b, 51t, 54t, 61 (all), 62t, 71t/ml/mr, 75tr, 77ml, 83bl, 93br/bm, 96 (all), 102 (all), 108t, 118b, 124m/b, 127tr, 135bl,136 (all), 137tr, 145m, 149tl/b, 154m, 155m. **Roland Brown/ Graeme Bell** 67t. **Roland Brown/Jack Burnicle** 16t/m, 42t/b, 43tl. **Roland Brown/Gold & Goose** 11tl, 42t/b, 34 (all), 35tr, 36b, 44t, 45tr, 53t, 103l 2 down/bl, 125b, 147b. **Roland Brown/Phil Masters** Back jacket bottom middle, 15b, 19b, 22t/m, 77r, 81mr/b, 103l 3 down, 112b, 113tl, 144t, 148b. **Roland Brown/Mac McDiarmid** 109b,

111b, 118t. **Roland Brown/Oli Tennent** 6, 17b, 18-9t, 23b, 37br, 45br, 47t/ml/b, 58-9b, 73tml, 74 (all), 92 (all), 93t/bl, 94t, 95tr/tl/m, 105b, 111tl/m, 110 (all), 116t, 139tl/tr, 146 (all), 149tr/m, 154t/b. **Jack Burnicle** 16b, 55bl, 72b. **Kel Edge** 38t, 65tl/b, 69tl, 81tl, 81t, 95bl, 99ml/mr, 113tr, 125ml, 133b, 139m 3 down, 141b, 145b, 158b, 159bl. **Gold & Goose** Back jacket top right. **John Freeman/ (c) Anness Publishing** 11tr, 24, 36t, 45bl, 78b, 79tl, 80b, 82, 85tl/tr, 87b, 94b, 97bl, 98-9b, 99t, 135t/m, 157tl. **Phil Masters** 18-9b, 25tr, 27t, 39m, 63b, 67m, 76 (all), 112t, 137b, 140t, 148t, 155b, 156, 157b. **Mac McDiarmid** 10b, 15tl/tr, 25m, 26 (all), 27bl/br, 30m, 117m/b, 38b, 39mt/mb, 41tr, 54b, 64 (all), 65tr, 69m, 71b, 72t, 79b, 100lb, 101l, 105tr, 107tl/tr, 109m, 117tl/tr, 123b, 131t, 134m/b, 139b, 142t, 143tl/b, 145tl/tr, 150 (all), 152m/b. **Don Morley** Front jacket, back jacket top left, top middle, bottom left, bottom right, 7, 9 (all), 11m, 12 (all), 13t/b, 15 (all), 17t, 19m, 20, 21 (all), 22b, 28 (all), 29 (all), 31(all), 32t, 33 (all), 35m/bl, 37tl/tr,

39tl/tr/2 down, 43tr/m, 45tl, 46t, 47mr, 48t/m, 49, 50 (all), 51ml/mr/b, 52m/b, 53bl/br, 55m/br, 57t/b, 59t/bl, 65m, 66t, 67br, 68b, 69b, 71mr, 73tr/m, 75bl/br, 77tl, 79tr, 80t, 83tl/tr/m/br, 81m/b, 85m/bl/br, 86t, 89tl, 91tr/b, 97br, 100t, 101tr/mr, 103br, 104 (all), 105tl/m, 106b, 107m/bl/br, 108b, 109t, 113bl, 114 (all), 115m/b, 116b, 117b, 119tl/mr/b, 120 (all), 121 tl/tr/b, 122 (all), 123t/ml/mr, 125tr, 127mr, 130b, 131b, 132b, 133t/m, 135br, 137tl, 140b, 141tl/tr/ml, 142b, 143tr, 144b, 147t/ml/mr, 151t/ml/lmr, 153tl/r 2 down/b, 155tr, 158t, 159t/bm/br. **Nick Nicholls** 55t, 119m, 127b, 155tl. **John Nutting** 81tr, 97t, 103tl, 113br, 119tr, 138 (all), 157tr/tm. **Garry Stuart** 58t, 59m/br, 60 (all), 62b, 63t/m, 66b, 86b, 87t/m, 88t, 89tr. **Phillip Tooth** 56. **Oli Tennent** Back flap, 52t, 78t, 98t, 139m 2 down. Thanks also to the PR departments of BMW, Ducati, Honda, Moto Guzzi, Kawasaki, Suzuki and Yamaha for their help in supplying photographs.

t=top, b=bottom, m=middle, l=left, r=right.

This edition published by Hermes House,
an imprint of Anness Publishing Limited
Hermes House, 88–89 Blackfriars Road,
London SE1 8HA

© Anness Publishing Limited 1996, 1999, 2002

Published in the USA by Hermes House, Anness Publishing Inc.
27 West 20th Street, New York, NY 10011

Publisher: Joanna Lorenz
Project Editor: Joanne Rippin
Designer: Michael Morey
Illustrator: Stephen Sweet

Previously published as part of a larger compendium, *The Encyclopedia of the Motorcycle*

1 3 5 7 9 10 8 6 4 2

Contents

INTRODUCTION

A – Z OF
MOTORCYCLES

The A-Z section that follows is a guide to the major manufacturers and the models they have produced since Gottlieb Daimler first fired-up Einspur back in 1885. No attempt has been made to cover all the makes: that would have been impossible. Motorcycling's history is littered with names of firms that built a few bikes and then went out of business, many of them before 1930. Names such as Abako, Abbotsford, ABC Scootamota, Abendsonne, Aberdale, Abe-Star.

The most important marques and their greatest hits, plus a few misses, are here, from AJS and Bimota to Yamaha and Zündapp. Between them they tell the story of an industry that has had many ups and downs, but which has produced many fine machines for the benefit of millions of riders worldwide. Some bikes have been cleverly engineered, others are simply beautiful to look at. The best have combined both style and performance, giving their riders the feeling of exhilaration and freedom that only a great motorcycle can provide.

AJS

■ BELOW *Although it looked uninspiring, the AJS Model 30 handled well and was comfortable and reliable.*

■ AJS MODEL 30

Like most AJS roadsters, the 600cc Model 30 of the late 1950s suffered from a case of dual personality. Almost exactly the same bike, differing only in paint colour, badges and exhaust system, was also sold as the Matchless G11 – a result of the Wolverhampton-based AJS firm having been taken over by Matchless of London in 1931. The combined firm in turn became part of Associated Motor Cycles (AMC) in 1938, but the AJS and Matchless names were retained and used in an attempt to attract the continued support of each of the brand's enthusiasts.

AJS had originally been founded by Albert John Stevens in Wolverhampton around the turn of the century, and won the Junior TT in 1914. But AJS's greatest racing feats came later, notably when Les Graham won the first ever 500cc world championship on the Porcupine twin in 1949.

The most popular AJS racebike was the single-cylinder 350cc 7R, known as the "Boy Racer". Introduced in 1948, the 7R was hugely successful and was later enlarged to 500cc to make the Matchless G50.

Most of AJS's roadsters were less spectacular singles and parallel twins such as the Model 30, whose 600cc engine had almost square dimensions, and gave a smoother ride than most other models. Peak output was only 33bhp but the twin was capable of cruising fairly smoothly at 70mph (112kph). Handling was predictable and made for a relaxed, comfortable bike over distances. The Model 30 was also well-made, reliable and economical. Unfortunately such attributes were not

AJS MODEL 30 (1957)

Engine	Aircooled 4-valve OHV pushrod parallel twin
Capacity	593cc (72 x 72.8mm)
Power	33bhp @ 6800rpm
Weight	180kg (396lb)
Top speed	95mph (152kph)

■ BELOW *AJS "Boy Racers" such as this 1954-model 7R/3 remained competitive at international level for many years.*

■ BELOW *Notable early AJS models included the 350cc "Big Port" single-cylinder racer of the 1920s.*

enough to keep AJS in business. Poor sales led to parent company AMC becoming part of Norton Villiers in 1967. Some AJS bikes were then built incorporating Norton parts, but they were not successful and the factory ceased production shortly afterwards.

OTHER MAKES

■ ABC
Best known of several ABCs in the 1920s was the 398cc flat-twin built by British aircraft firm Sopwith. Regarded as the predecessor of the first BMW, the engine's unreliability led to ABC's collapse.

■ ACE
American Bill Henderson set up ACE after selling his Henderson firm to the Schwinn cycle company in 1917, and produced bikes with a similar in-line four-cylinder layout. Best known was the XP-4, which set a record speed of 130mph (209kph) in 1923. Rights were later sold to Indian, who built a similar four.

■ ADLER
Germany's Adler built motorbikes for a short time from 1902, then concentrated on cars and bicycles before making a comeback in 1949. The firm's most popular model was the M250, a twin-cylinder two-stroke roadster released in

■ ABOVE *Four-cylinder ACE racers such as this were among the world's fastest bikes in 1923.*

1953. Adlers were ridden successfully in road races and enduros, but sales declined. Finally in 1958 the firm was taken over by the Grundig Corporation, who abandoned bikes to concentrate on producing typewriters.

■ AERMACCHI
The former aircraft factory at Varese in northern Italy built some fine 250 and 350cc single-cylinder four-strokes in the 1950s and 1960s, most notably racebikes such as the 100mph (160kph) Ala d'Oro 250 introduced in 1959. Aermacchi turned to two-strokes after being bought by AMF Harley-Davidson in the 1960s. Walter Villa rode Varese-built Harleys to four 250 and 350cc world titles between 1974 and 1976, but two years later the firm was declared bankrupt and sold to Cagiva.

■ ABOVE *A 350cc Aermacchi single from the mid-1960s in racing action.*

APRILIA

■ **BELOW** *Road-going RS250's massive twin-spar aluminium frame held a tuned Suzuki V-twin engine.*

■ APRILIA RS250

In recent years Aprilia has been one of the world's most dynamic and fastest growing motorcycle manufacturers, with an aggressive approach to design and performance typified by the RS250. Essentially a road-going replica of the two-stroke Grand Prix bike on which Italian idol Max Biaggi won the 1994 250cc world championship, the RS combined a high-revving two-stroke engine with a massive twin-beam aluminium frame, top-class cycle parts and streamlined, racetrack-inspired styling.

Its engine was a subtly redesigned version of the V-twin powerplant from Suzuki's RGV250, and produced a maximum of 70bhp. With its aggressive

APRILIA RS250 (1995)	
Engine	Watercooled 90-degree V-twin two-stroke
Capacity	249cc (56 x 50.6mm)
Power	70bhp @ 11,900rpm
Weight	141kg (310lb)
Top speed	130mph (209kph)

riding position, peaky powerplant and ultra-light weight, the RS came closer than any other bike to providing Grand Prix style thrills on the road. Given enough frantic revving through the gears the Aprilia screamed towards a top speed of 130mph (208kph), and in the

■ **LEFT** *Its light weight and superb chassis made the RS250 almost unbeatable for fast cornering.*

■ **BELOW** *The title-winning 250cc Grand Prix racebike provided inspiration for the RS250 roadster.*

bends its superb suspension, powerful brakes and sticky tyres combined to make the RS250 almost unbeatable.

Aprilia certainly proved difficult to beat on the track in 1994, winning both the 250 and 125cc world titles with Biaggi and Japan's Kazuto Sakata. In all, it was quite a year for the small company from Noale, near Venice in northern Italy. Aprilia also began building the single-cylinder F650 for BMW, and announced that production of its own bikes had doubled in three years to 100,000 units. Yet it was only in 1973 that Ivano Beggio had taken control of the family bicycle firm and moved into the motorcycle business.

Beggio attributes much of Aprilia's subsequent success to an unusual policy of manufacturing virtually none of its components in-house. Instead, Aprilia relies on a network of suppliers for parts that are assembled at Noale. Also unusually, over a quarter of Aprilia's workforce of 500 is employed in racing or research and development. Racing has always been vital to Aprilia, providing important technical feedback as well as publicity.

Aprilia's roadbike production has traditionally been based on two-stroke sports and trail bikes of 125cc capacity, with names like Futura, Extrema and Pegaso. That went a step further in 1995 with the arrival of the RS250. At the same time Beggio was also planning an attack on the World Superbike Championship, and revealed a large-capacity four-stroke V-twin engine designed to power a range of sportsbikes and cruisers.

OTHER MAKES

■ **AJW**
British firm AJW built numerous parallel twins and singles dating back to the 1920s, and carried on after the Second World War with its best-known model, the 500cc, JAP-engined Grey Fox.

■ **ABOVE** *In the 1930s AJW built 500cc singles, such as this one, using engines from Stevens and JAP.*

■ **AMAZONAS**
Notable for its size but not for its performance, the Brazilian-made Amazonas of the mid-1980s was powered by the flat-four VW car engine. Its astonishing vital statistics were an engine capacity of 1584cc, producing just 56bhp that needed to propel a massive 385kg (848lb).

■ **RIGHT** *Aprilia's 1995-model Motò 6.5 roadster was created by brilliant French designer Philippe Starck.*

■ **OPPOSITE** *The RS250's colours matched those of the 400cc V-twin raced in 500cc Grands Prix by Loris Reggiani.*

ARIEL

■ ARIEL RED HUNTER

One of the oldest manufacturers of all, Ariel was known for its bicycles before they started to build motorcycles around the turn of the century. By the early 1930s, the firm from Selly Oak in the Midlands was one of Britain's most influential, and at that time employed Edward Turner, Val Page and Bert Hopwood – who would eventually

■ LEFT *Ariel's 650cc Huntmaster parallel twin, introduced in 1954, was popular for both solo and sidecar use.*

■ BELOW *A 1954 redesign failed to make the 500cc KH twin a success.*

ARIEL VH500 RED HUNTER (1937)

Engine	Aircooled 2-valve OHV pushrod single
Capacity	497cc (81.8 x 85mm)
Power	26bhp @ 5600rpm
Weight	170kg (375lb)
Top speed	82mph (131kph)

become known as three of the British bike industry's greatest designers.

Ariel hit financial problems during the 1930s and the factory was closed for a time until Jack Sangster, son of founder Charles, bought the firm and restarted production of Page-designed single-cylinder four-strokes including the Red Hunter. These were handsome machines, built in 350 and 500cc sizes, that were produced from 1932 to the late 1950s, and were even successful in sidecar trials into the 1970s. Sammy Miller's successful GOV132 trials bike was based on a 1955 Red Hunter 500.

A late 1930s Red Hunter 500 was among the best bikes of its day, capable of well over 75mph (120kph) and reliable with it. Handling provided by

the combination of girder forks and rigid rear end was respectable too; rear suspension was not to be introduced until 1939. The Hunter was refined throughout the 1930s, gained telescopic forks when production recommenced after the Second World War and was kept going with an alloy cylinder head and new frame in the early 1950s.

After the firm's sale to BSA in 1944, Ariel built two main types of twin, firstly the softly-tuned 500cc KH, which was introduced in 1949 but sold poorly. More powerful and successful was the Huntmaster, which was powered by a slightly modified version of the 650cc twin-cylinder engine from BSA's A10. There was more to the Huntmaster than mere badge engineering, since most parts, including the frame, were its own.

The result was a pleasant bike, good for 100mph (160kph) that was particularly popular with sidecar enthusiasts in the late 1950s.

If Ariel's most famous bike is undoubtedly the Square Four, then the bravest must be the Leader, the innovative, fully enclosed 250cc two-stroke released in 1959. With an 18bhp, twin-cylinder engine based on that of the German Adler, a pressed steel frame, effective weather protection and optional panniers, the Leader was intended to be a proper motorcycle with the convenience of a scooter.

The Leader actually worked rather well, with a top speed of about 70mph (112kph) and excellent handling. But the public didn't take to it, partly because the new Mini car offered cheap

four-wheeled travel, and the bike had temperamental starting and poor brakes and finish. Ariel later stripped off the bodywork to produce the Arrow, tuning the engine to 20bhp to produce Super Sports and Golden Arrow versions. But although the Arrow sold quite well it wasn't enough to save Ariel, and the firm eventually ceased trading in 1967.

■ RIGHT *Leader was a sales flop.*

ARIEL

ARIEL SQUARE FOUR

One of the most famous roadsters of all, Ariel's Square Four was also one of the longest lived, remaining in production in various forms from 1931 to 1958. The Square Four, whose powerplant was effectively a pair of geared-together parallel twins, was designed by Edward Turner shortly after the future Triumph boss had joined Ariel in 1928. The Four's capacity of 500cc was soon afterwards increased to 600cc and then 997cc. In all three forms the "Squariel" was superbly smooth, but suffered from overheating problems with its rear cylinders. Although the biggest model was capable of more than 100mph (160kph), its performance was severely handicapped by its excessive weight.

After the Second World War the Square Four was comprehensively updated, first with a lighter aluminium engine and then, in 1954, with a new cylinder head and striking four-pipe exhaust system. By this time the Ariel had also gained telescopic front forks and plunger rear suspension. Despite this, the heavy Four was a soggy handler. Even in its final, more sophisticated guise the engine was prone to overheat. But the Square Four's smoothness, relaxed high-speed cruising ability, comfort and looks made the bike much loved by those who could afford one.

ARIEL SQUARE FOUR (1958)	
Engine	Aircooled 8-valve OHV pushrod square four
Capacity	997cc (65 x 75mm)
Power	45bhp @ 5500rpm
Weight	211kg (465lb)
Top speed	105mph (168kph)

■ **BELOW** *The looks of the later Square Fours, such as this 1958 model, were enhanced by a four-pipe exhaust system.*

■ OPPOSITE
*Handling was never
the big, heavy
Square Four's
forte, but it could
still be made to
corner rapidly.*

■ BELOW *Square
Fours such as this
model from 1937
were supremely
smooth and good
for almost 100mph
(160kph).*

■ RIGHT AND
BELOW RIGHT *The
997cc Square Four
from 1937 – with
instruments set into
fuel tank –
produced 36bhp.*

OTHER MAKES

■ ARMSTRONG

The motorcycle arm of British car components giant Armstrong produced motocross, trials, road racing and military bikes in the 1980s, after taking over Barton Engineering and CCM. Most were powered by engines from Rotax of Austria. Armstrong's CF250 road-racer, introduced in 1983, featured a tandem-twin Rotax engine in an innovative twin-spar carbon fibre frame. Niall Mackenzie and Donnie McLeod dominated British racing, and scored some impressive results in Grands Prix. Armstrong also built a very successful single-cylinder, four-stroke military bike, rights to which were later sold to Harley-Davidson.

■ ATK

Utah-based ATK made its reputation building motocross bikes with both two-stroke and four-stroke engines, most of which were sold in the States. Following a

■ ABOVE *Future 500cc Grand Prix star Niall Mackenzie rose to prominence on Armstrong's rapid 250cc twin.*

change of ownership, the firm introduced a pair of purposeful street legal Dirt Sports machines in 1994.

■ BAKKER

Many superb specials and racebikes have emerged from Nico

Bakker's workshop in northern Holland, most with innovative chassis, and with engines ranging from Yamaha's TZ350 to BMW and Harley-Davidson four-strokes. His radical QCS (Quick Change System) sportsbike, most recently powered by Yamaha's FZR1000 engine, used an advanced non-telescopic front suspension system. Bakker has also done much chassis development work for manufacturers including BMW and Laverda.

■ BELOW *Bakker's Bomber used BMW's R1100 flat-twin engine.*

BENELLI

■ BENELLI 750 SEI

With its smart styling, Italian racing-red paintwork and the unique attraction of its six-cylinder engine – emphasized by an array of gleaming chromed exhaust pipes – the Benelli 750 Sei looked set to be a world beater when it was launched

BENELLI 750 SEI (1975)

Engine	Aircooled 12-valve SOHC transverse six
Capacity	748cc (56 x 50.6mm)
Power	71bhp @ 8900rpm
Weight	220kg (485lb) dry
Top speed	118mph (189kph)

in 1975. Instead the Sei turned out to be softly tuned and no faster than Honda's CB750-four of six years earlier. Its modest performance led to the Benelli being overshadowed by more powerful superbikes, particularly its Italian rivals

from Ducati, Guzzi and Laverda.

Not that the Sei was a bad bike, indeed in most respects it was a very good one. The engine, although criticized for closely resembling one-and-a-half Honda CB500 units, was commendably narrow for a six. The

■ LEFT *The Sei was supremely smooth and comfortable, but its straight-line performance was unexceptional.*

■ BELOW AND BOTTOM *The Sei's big aircooled engine and its six exhaust pipes dominate from every angle.*

■ RIGHT
*Benelli's 250cc
four was raced
successfully by
Renzo Pasolini and
Kel Carruthers in
the 1960s.*

three dual-manifold Dell'Orto carburettors allowed room for the rider's knees, always a potential problem with a six, and the engine made plenty of smooth midrange power. But the maximum output of 71bhp gave a top speed of just 120mph (193kph), and even the Sei's excellent handling, roadholding and braking could not make up for that in the eyes of riders looking for an expensive Italian superbike.

The Sei's lack of blood and thunder was surprising given Benelli's racing pedigree. The firm was founded by six

Benelli brothers from Pesaro, and produced its first bike in 1921. Tonino, the youngest brother, was the first racer to put Benelli on the map, notably on a 175cc four-stroke prepared by big brother Giovanni in 1937. Tonino retired shortly afterwards but Benelli's bikes continued to win, culminating in Dario Ambrosini's victory in the 250cc world championship in 1950.

Ambrosini's death a year later shook Benelli but the firm eventually returned to racing and in 1960 built a four-cylinder 250cc machine. Italian stars

Tarquinio Provini and Renzo Pasolini won many races on it through the 1960s but it was Australian Kel Carruthers who did best of all, winning the 250cc world championship in 1969.

Sadly, track success was not matched in the showrooms and shortly afterwards the Benelli family sold out to Argentinian car baron Alejandro de Tomaso. He aimed to relaunch Benelli with the 750 Sei, but neither that nor the slightly more powerful 900cc version that followed it could recapture the Pesaro firm's former glory.

OTHER MAKES

■ BARIGO

Founded by Patrick Barigault at La Roch-elle on the west coast of France, Barigo is a small firm with a background in the peculiarly French supermoto, a combina-tion of road racing and motocross. In 1992 Barigo produced the Supermotard roadster –basically a street legal version of the firm's competition machine–with a 600cc Rotax single-cylinder engine, aluminium twin-beam frame, long-travel suspension and supermoto styling. Two years later came the Onixa, which combined a similar motor and frame with sportsbike parts and striking, fully-faired bodywork.

■ LEFT
*Barigo's 600cc
Onixa sportster
looked peculiar
but was very
light and
handled well.*

BIMOTA

■ BIMOTA SB6

Seventeen years and a gulf in technology separated Bimota's 1994 model SB6 from its predecessor the SB2, yet the two bikes had much more in common than the fact that each was powered by a four-cylinder Suzuki motor. The GSX-R1100-engined SB6 featured a curvaceous full fairing, state-of-the-art frame design, a self-supporting seat unit, top-quality cycle parts – and was arguably the world's most desirable sportsbike. Exactly the same had been true of the GS750-powered SB2 back in 1977.

The gap between the two bikes' release ensured that their performance was very different. The SB6's 1074cc watercooled, 16-valve engine, tuned

BIMOTA SB6 (1994)

Engine	Watercooled 16-valve DOHC transverse four
Capacity	1074cc (75.5 x 60mm)
Power	156bhp @ 10,000rpm
Weight	190kg (418lb)
Top speed	175mph (280kph)

with an exhaust system that curved up to twin silencers in the tailpiece, produced a claimed 156bhp and rocketed the Bimota to over 170mph (273kph). The impeccably rigid aluminium twin-spar Straight Connection Technology frame, massive 46mm (1.8in) diameter forks,

■ ABOVE *A strong aluminium frame, plus top-class suspension and tyres, gave the SB6 razor-sharp handling.*

■ RIGHT *With its sculpted bodywork and state-of-the-art chassis, Bimota's SB2 was a sensation in 1977.*

■ LEFT *The stylish and rapid SB6, powered by Suzuki's GSX-R1100 engine, was a great success for Bimota.*

OTHER MAKES

■ BETA
Italian firm Beta built a rapid 175cc roadster in the late 1950s, but in recent years has concentrated on the off-road market, particularly trials bikes.

■ BFG
Powered by the 70bhp, 1300cc flat-four engine normally found in a Citroën GS car, the French-built BFG was intended

as a grand tourer. Strange styling and excess weight meant that sales were limited mainly to the French police, and BFG went bust in the mid-1980s.

■ BIANCHI
Best known for some impressive Grand Prix performances in the early 1960s, Bianchi built bicycles before becoming one of the first Italian motorcycle manufacturers in 1897. Bianchi won many races in the 1920s, built a spectacular supercharged four-cylinder 500cc racer in 1938, and sold motocross bikes as well as small-capacity roadsters before motorcycle production ended in 1967.

■ LEFT *In the early 1960s Bianchi produced both racing bikes, and roadsters such as this 300cc MT61.*

sophisticated Öhlins shock, fat Michelin radial tyres and big Brembo brake discs gave superb cornering and stopping power. The SB2 came from a much earlier era of bike design, yet was considered even more exotic in its day.

Bimota was formed in Rimini, Italy in 1973 by Messrs Bianchi, Morri and Tamburini – the name of the company being derived from the first two letters of each name. The SB2 was the firm's first

purpose-built roadster, and held its 75bhp aircooled GS750 motor in a tubular steel frame. Suspension, brakes and tyres were the best available, and the seat-tank unit's fibreglass was lined with aluminium, meaning no rear subframe was needed. The Bimota's 130mph (209kph) top speed and heavy handling could not compare with the performance of its SB6 successor, but in 1977 the SB2 was the ultimate roadster.

BMW

■ BMW R60/2

In recent years BMW has produced bikes with one, three and four cylinders, but the German firm's name is synonymous with flat-twins. The very first BMW motorcycle, the R32 of 1923, was powered by a boxer engine that produced 8bhp at 3300rpm and used shaft final drive. The R32 was rather expensive – but it was cleverly designed, nicely finished and sold well. Some things really don't change.

Among the most popular BMW twins during the 1950s and 1960s were the 600cc R60 and its successor the R60/2, which was launched in 1960. These models, and also the slightly slower 500cc R50 and R50/2 bikes of the same period, were hugely successful due to their relaxed, fuss-free nature, reliability and general ease of use. The R60/2 used a slightly tuned version of the 28bhp

BMW R60/2 (1960)	
Engine	Aircooled 4-valve pushrod flat-twin
Capacity	494cc (68 x 68mm)
Power	26bhp @ 5800rpm
Weight	195kg (430lb)
Top speed	87mph (139kph)

aircooled boxer motor from the R60, which gave superbly smooth running and a top speed of about 90mph (145kph). Although BMW had been among the first firms to use telescopic forks in the 1930s, the R60/2 was fitted with leading-link Earles forks which were particularly well suited to sidecar work. Heavy steering and soft suspension at both ends made the 60/2 ill-suited to sporty solo riding, but the

BMW had few equals for comfortable long-distance touring.

BMW has had little involvement in top level competition in recent years, but has a long and impressive history of racing and record-breaking. One of the most famous early stars was Ernst Henne, who set a number of speed records on streamlined, supercharged boxers in the 1930s. Schorsch Meier became the first foreign rider to win an Isle of Man TT when he took the 1939 Senior race on a supercharged 500cc flat-twin. Works BMW pilot Walter Zeller won many international races for BMW in the 1950s, finishing second in the 500cc world championship in 1956. And BMW flat-twins dominated sidecar racing for two decades, winning 19 out of 21 world championships between 1954 and 1974 with drivers including Max Deubel and Klaus Enders.

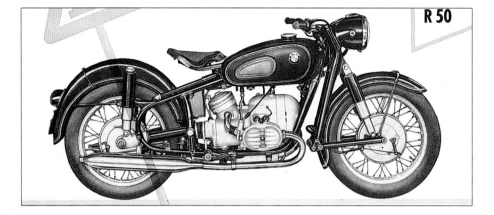

■ LEFT *The 494cc R50/2, seen here in 1955 with a single saddle, shared many parts with the 60/2.*

■ BELOW LEFT *Schorsch Meier's 1939 TT-winning supercharged twin had a top speed of over 125mph (201kph).*

■ BELOW *Fritz Scheidegger's world titles in 1965 and 1966 continued a long run of BMW sidecar success.*

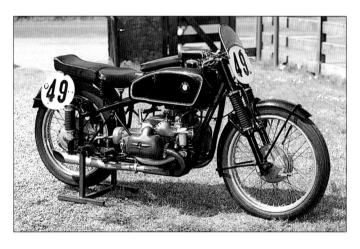

■ RIGHT
This 500cc, 12bhp R52 flat-twin dates from 1928, the first year BMW fitted lights as standard.

■ OPPOSITE
With its Earles forks, smooth 30bhp engine and all-round comfort, the R60/2 made a fine tourer.

BMW

■ BMW R90S

BMW's traditional flat-twins were gradually refined over the years and reached new heights of performance and desirability with the R90S of 1974. The basis of the R90S was the familiar 898cc boxer lump from the R90/6, tuned slightly to give 67bhp at 7000rpm. To the normal specification the R90S added a neat bikini fairing, stylish smoked paintwork, twin front disc brakes and even the luxury of a clock in the dashboard.

The R90S couldn't match the sheer

■ RIGHT
Although it was built for comfort as well as speed, the R90S was a match for most bikes in the corners.

■ BELOW
With its fairing and smoked orange paintwork the R90S had the looks to match its superb performance.

■ ABOVE *Increased compression ratio and 38mm Dell'Orto carburettors gave the R90S an output of 67bhp.*

■ OPPOSITE *The stylish and versatile F650 accounted for over 25 per cent of BMW's production in 1994.*

BMW R90S (1974)

Engine	Aircooled 4-valve OHV pushrod flat-twin
Capacity	898cc (90 x 70.6mm)
Power	67bhp @ 7000rpm
Weight	215kg (474lb)
Top speed	125mph (201kph)

■ RIGHT
The sophisticated,
fine-handling
R1100RS sports-
tourer heralded a
new era for BMW
flat-twins.

power of mid-1970s Japanese superbikes such as Kawasaki's four-cylinder Z1, or the handling finesse of Italian sportsters from Ducati and Moto Guzzi. But the German bike accelerated smoothly to a top speed of 125mph (201kph), handled very respectably, and was superbly comfortable, well-finished and reliable. In 1974 the R90S was more than twice as expensive as Honda's CB750 in most markets – but in many riders' opinion, BMW's majestic sports-tourer was simply the best production motorcycle in the world.

In the early 1980s the future looked bleak for the flat-twins, as BMW released its new range of watercooled K-series fours and triples. But demand for the traditional twins remained strong, several models were reprieved and updated, and BMW's management thought again. In 1993, came the new-generation boxer, the R1100RS, powered by a 1085cc fuel-injected, air/oilcooled, four-valves-per-cylinder, high-cam motor producing 90bhp.

The R1100RS's chassis was noteworthy, too, because it incorporated Telelever front suspension. Instead of telescopic forks, the system consisted of hollow fork legs, a horizontal arm pivoting on the engine, and a single suspension unit. Telelever worked well, giving good handling and a smooth ride, and the rest of the RS was equally impressive. With plenty of mid-range power, a 135mph (217kph) top speed, a protective fairing, generous fuel range and powerful, anti-lock brakes, the

R1100RS was a sports-tourer in the finest BMW boxer tradition.

BMW's tradition of building single-cylinder bikes dates back to the 250cc R39 of 1925, and singles were produced – effectively by mounting one cylinder of a twin vertically – until R27 production was halted in 1967. The F650 single, introduced in 1994, was an altogether different machine. The first chain-driven model in BMW's 70-year

history, the F650 also defied convention by being assembled in Italy, by Aprilia, and by using a watercooled, 652cc engine built by Rotax of Austria. The chassis was derived from that of Aprilia's Pegaso trail bike, and gave taut handling well suited to the BMW's 100mph (160kph) performance. The F650 worked well as a versatile and relatively inexpensive roadster, and its sales success surprised even BMW.

BMW

■ BMW K1

With its brightly-coloured, all-enveloping bodywork, the K1 was a startling bike by any manufacturer's standards when it was launched in 1989, let alone by the standards of traditionally conservative BMW. In conjunction with the huge front mudguard, the K1's fairing and large rear section combined to give a wind-cheating shape unmatched even by Japanese sportsbikes.

Behind the plastic was a tuned, 16-valve version of the watercooled,

BMW K1 (1989)	
Engine	Watercooled 16-valve DOHC longitudinal four
Capacity	987cc (67 x 70mm)
Power	100bhp @ 8000rpm
Weight	234kg (468lb) wet
Top speed	145mph (233kph)

987cc four-cylinder engine that had been introduced five years earlier in the K100. The K-series four aligned its

cylinders horizontally, in contrast to the transverse layout favoured by the Japanese. In K1 form the fuel-injected four produced 100bhp, sufficient to send the aerodynamically efficient BMW to a top speed of over 140mph (225kph). A strong steel frame, based on that of the K100, firm suspension (with the Paralever system to combat the effect of the drive-shaft) and powerful triple-disc braking gave good handling and stopping power. The K1 was too big and heavy to be a true sportsbike, but it did much to boost BMW's image.

■ BELOW *With its aggressive styling, the K1 was a radical departure for traditionally conservative BMW.*

■ LEFT
BMW's K-series engine held its cylinders horizontally, and in K1 form had 16 valves.

■ BELOW
The K1 was far less sporty than its looks suggested, but its handling was still exceptionally good.

OTHER MAKES

■ BÖHMERLAND

Notable for its vast length and for being designed to carry three people, the Böhmerland was produced in Czechoslovakia between 1923 and 1939. Designed and built by Albin Liebisch, the Böhmerland was powered by a 600cc, 16bhp single-cylinder engine. As well as the long wheelbase "Langtouren", with its rear pannier fuel tanks, there was a shorter Jubilee model, and a sportier bike called the Racer.

■ BOSS HOSS

Originally named Boss Hog until Harley-Davidson objected, and powered by America's ubiquitous Chevrolet V-eight engine – typically with a capacity approaching six litres and output of 300bhp – the Boss Hoss was arguably the biggest, heaviest and most powerful bike, but not the most sensible, in series production. Final drive was by chain and there was only one gear: fast forward. Claimed top speed was over 150mph (241kph) but the Hoss's handling, with 450kg (992lb) of weight and a square-section rear tyre, made for just as much excitement. Over 150 of these huge beasts had been produced by Tennessee-based Boss Hoss firm by the early 1990s.

■ ABOVE The amazing Böhmerland had a top speed of over 70mph (112kph).

■ ABOVE AND RIGHT
Its awesome Chevy V-eight powerplant made the Boss Hoss very fast – in a straight line!

BRITTEN

■ BRITTEN V-1000

Impressive displays in international twin-cylinder races in recent seasons confirmed the Britten V-twin's status as one of the world's most exotic and brilliantly engineered motorbikes. Designed and almost totally hand-built by New Zealander John Britten and his small team, the Britten was powered by a watercooled, fuel-injected 60-degree V-twin motor. After the original V-1000 had made its mark at Daytona in 1991, its engine was enlarged to 1108cc, producing a phenomenal 171bhp. To allow the bike to compete in Superbike racing, Britten then developed a new V-1000 with a 985cc, short-stroke engine.

The rigid power unit acted as the V-1000's frame, supporting girder forks and the huge rear swing-arm, both of which were formed from lightweight Kevlar and carbon fibre. Front and rear

suspension systems were multi-adjustable and used Öhlins shocks. The rear unit was situated in front of the engine for optimum cooling. The Britten

BRITTEN V-1000 (1995)	
Engine	Watercooled dohc 8-valve 60-degree V-twin
Capacity	985cc (99 x 64mm)
Power	155bhp @ 12,400rpm
Weight	145kg (320lb) wet
Top speed	185mph (296kph)

featured an advanced, computerized engine-management system that recorded and could adjust the engine's performance as it ran. To top it all, the V-1000 was beautifully styled; its narrow width and sensuous curves contributed to recorded speeds of more than 180mph (289kph) at Daytona.

As well as the bikes raced successfully by Britten's own riders including Paul Lewis and Andrew

Stroud, small numbers of production racebikes were sold for sizeable sums of money. The V-1000's elaborate construction made the prospect of a road-going version appear remote.

In 1995, when the racebike was again successful at Daytona, John Britten's collaboration with the Indian marque's new Australian owner, Maurits Hayim-Langridge, looked likely to result in elements of the V-1000 being incorporated in Indian streetbikes due for release within a few years. When Britten tragically died of cancer only six months later, at the age of 45, the motorcycle world lost one of its greatest engineering talents.

■ ABOVE *Its engine-management system allowed the Britten, ridden here by Jim Moodie, to be fine-tuned to suit the conditions.*

■ OPPOSITE *The sculpted V-1000 was one of the most beautiful bikes ever built, as well as one of the fastest.*

OTHER MAKES

■ BRIDGESTONE

Motorcycle production was never any more than a sideline for the Bridgestone rubber company, which remains a major tyre manufacturer to this day. But in the 1950s and 1960s Bridgestone built a range of bikes, from mopeds to twin-cylinder two-stroke sportsters, the best of which was the 350GTR. Powered by a disc-valve, parallel-twin engine that produced a claimed 40bhp, the GTR was a quick and stylish motorcycle that was capable of over 90mph (145kph).

The six-speed Bridgestone was a sophisticated machine when it was launched on the American market in 1966. Its rubber-mounted motor was reasonably smooth, and its blend of steel twin-downtube frame, gaitered forks and twin shocks gave good handling with a plush ride. But the high price limited export sales and at the end of that year Bridgestone, who had declined to take on important tyre customers Honda, Kawasaki, Suzuki and Yamaha by selling bikes on the home market, quit motorcycle manufacture altogether.

■ LEFT AND INSET *The disc-valve 350GTR was fast and refined, but Bridgestone abandoned it to concentrate on tyre production.*

BROUGH SUPERIOR

■ BROUGH SUPERIOR SS100

George Brough combined his own frames with bought-in engines and other parts to produce bikes which were innovative, exclusive, expensive and, above all, fast. Never one to sell his products short, he named his first machine the Superior to the displeasure of his motorcycle engineer father, William Brough, who built flat-twins and who commented that he supposed his was now to be known as the Inferior.

But superior George's bikes were – as they proved with a string of race wins and speed records in the 1920s and 1930s – ridden by Brough himself and other legendary figures such as Eric Fernihough, Freddie Dixon and Bert Le Vack. The machines built by the small

■ LEFT *By 1939,
the SS100 was
powered by a 50-
degree Matchless
V-twin engine,
fitted with a four
speed gearbox.*

■ BELOW *Earlier SS100s, such as this
1926 example, used powerplants from JAP
of Tottenham, north London.*

■ BOTTOM *Had not the Second World
War intervened, Brough's flat-four Dream
might have proved an outstanding machine.*

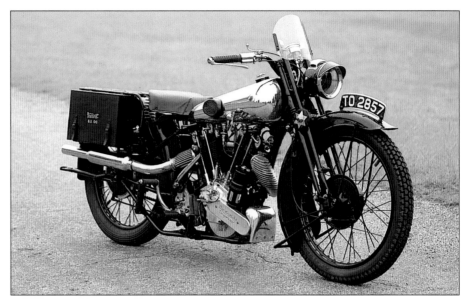

BROUGH SUPERIOR SS100 (1939)

Engine	Aircooled 4-valve OHV pushrod 50-degree V-twin
Capacity	988cc (85.5 x 86mm)
Power	45bhp @ 5000rpm
Weight	180kg (396lb) dry
Top speed	100mph (160kph)

team from Nottingham were regarded by many as the best in the world. When *The Motor Cycle* summed up a test by saying a Superior was the Rolls Royce of motorcycles, Brough seized on the line for his advertising – and Rolls didn't object.

The SS100, produced between 1925 and 1940, was Brough's most famous model. It was powered initially by a 980cc V-twin from JA Prestwich (JAP), the big engine-making firm from north London, and came with a signed guarantee from Brough that the bike had been timed at over 100mph (160kph) for a quarter of a mile (0.4 kilometres). Brochures also boasted of the hands-off stability at speeds of 95mph (152kph).

Fewer than 400 SS100s were built, most using the JAP engine but the last 100 or so models powered by a Matchless V-twin. The bike's specification was constantly changed, with the result that no two SS100s were identical. Optional rear suspension was

introduced in 1928, foot gearchange in 1935 and a four-speed Norton gearbox a year later. Brough's numerous innovations included flyscreens, twin headlamps, crashbars and panniers.

TE Shaw, alias Lawrence of Arabia, owned a series of Superiors (the last of which cost him his life in a crash), each of which he fitted with a special stainless steel petrol tank.

The Brough Superior that might have topped even the SS100 was the Dream, an exotic 990cc flat-four roadster that George Brough revealed in late 1938. Its engine featured twin crankshafts, linked by gears, and a firing arrangement that made it supremely smooth. Development of the promising Dream was halted when the Second World War broke out, and Brough Superior production was never restarted.

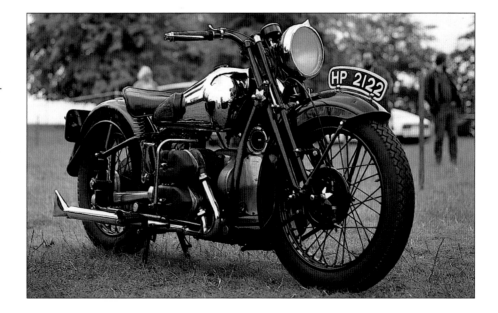

BSA

■ **LEFT**
A 500cc Gold Star with clip-on bars was ideal for rapid road riding in the 1950s and 1960s.

■ **BSA GOLD STAR DBD34**

For most of its life the Birmingham Small Arms Company was Britain's biggest motorcycle manufacturer, and in the years after the Second World War it was the largest in the world, producing over 75,000 bikes in some years during the 1950s. At that time BSA was an industrial giant, involved in producing guns, taxi-cabs and metal plate, and had also taken over Ariel and Sunbeam.

The firm's origins in armaments manufacture stretched back to 1863. Bicycle production followed in the 1880s and the Small Heath factory built its first motorcycle, powered by a Minerva engine, in 1905. BSA's reputation grew, notably with a series of reliable and successful V-twins in the 1920s.

BSA's best-loved early model was the S27, universally known as the Sloper

■ **BELOW AND BOTTOM** *Lean, functional and stylish, the DBD34 did the most to make the Gold Star badge famous.*

BSA GOLD STAR DBD34 (1956)

Engine	Aircooled 2-valve OHV pushrod single
Capacity	499cc (85 x 88mm)
Power	42bhp @ 7000rpm
Weight	159kg (350lb)
Top speed	110mph (177kph)

■ BELOW *This 1930s Champion spark plug advertisement featured the Sloper in an unflattering manner.*

■ LEFT
Over 125,000 of BSA's 500cc M20 singles were supplied to allied forces during the Second World War.

■ BELOW LEFT
This off-road Gold Star competed successfully in the International Six Days Trial in 1954.

■ BOTTOM
Slopers such as this model from the early 1930s were refined, quiet and good for 65mph (104kph).

due to its angled-forward single cylinder. Introduced with a 500cc engine in 1927, and later available in 350 to 595cc versions, the Sloper was stylish, sophisticated and notably quiet. It quickly became popular and was frequently updated through its ten years in production.

The Second World War was a particularly busy time for the BSA factory which, despite suffering heavy bomb damage that claimed 53 workers' lives, produced huge numbers of both guns and bikes.

The most famous BSA was the legendary Gold Star single, which was hugely successful as a roadster and as a competition bike in road racing, motocross and trials in the 1950s. The "Goldie" had its origins in 1937, when racer Walter Handley earned a Brooklands Gold Star award for lapping the banked track at over 100mph (160kph) on BSA's 500cc Empire Star. The next year's model was named Gold Star in recognition, and after a break for

the War it was relaunched, initially as a 350. Several tuning options were available, with power outputs ranging from 18bhp for the trials version, to over 30bhp for the track racer. Each bike was supplied with a factory certificate testifying to the machine's power.

Numerous revisions kept the Gold Star in top position throughout the 1950s. The archetypal model was the 500cc

DBD34 introduced in 1956, with its clip-on handlebars, polished tank and finned engine. An open-mouthed Amal carburettor and swept-back exhaust combined to give 110mph (177kph) top speed. The Gold Star dominated the Isle of Man Clubmans TT in that year and was successful in many unofficial burn-ups, remaining prized as a café racer after production ended in 1963.

B S A

■ BSA 650cc A10

BSA built two main versions of the trademark British parallel twin: the 500cc A7, which was introduced in 1946 and updated five years later, and the 650cc A10 that appeared in 1950. Both the A7 and A10 were sold in many forms in the 1950s, earning a reputation more for oil-tightness, economy and reliability than for looks or performance. In 1962 they were replaced by the 500cc A50 and the 650cc A65, which featured updates including a unit-construction engine and gearbox.

The original A10 was the Golden Flash, whose flexible, 35bhp single-camshaft engine gave a top speed approaching 100mph (160kph). In 1954 the Flash was updated with swing-arm rear suspension, instead of the old plunger design. Other A10s including

■ BELOW *The 646cc A10 of the mid-1950s was a handsome machine, and a big-selling success for BSA.*

BSA 650cc A10 GOLDEN FLASH (1958)

Engine	Aircooled 4-valve OHV pushrod parallel twin
Capacity	646cc (70 x 84mm)
Power	34bhp @ 5750rpm
Weight	195kg (430lb)
Top speed	96mph (154kph)

the Super Flash and Road Rocket provided a little more power and speed, and in 1958 BSA produced the A10S Super Rocket, with a 43bhp engine and top speed of 105mph (168kph).

The best and rarest of the bunch was the Rocket Gold Star introduced in 1962. This consisted of a slightly tuned Super Rocket engine in a frame based on that of the Gold Star single. Forks, brakes and wheels also came from the

■ OPPOSITE PAGE, TOP *This A65L Lightning twin provided good performance by mid-1960s' standards.*

■ LEFT *John Cooper rode BSA's 750cc triple to some famous victories.*

■ ABOVE *BSA's smaller twin was the 500cc A7, like this 1956-model Shooting Star.*

Gold Star, and the twin featured a close-ratio gearbox, rearset footrests and a siamesed exhaust system. The result was the fastest and best handling A10. In recent years the Rocket Gold Star's higher value has led to fakes being built by fitting the more common Super Rocket with special parts.

BSA's last great roadster was the 750cc Rocket Three triple, which appeared at the same time as the Triumph Trident in 1969. The two models shared a 58bhp engine that owed more to Triumph than BSA, although the Rocket Three unit was angled at 15 degrees in a different twin-downtube frame. Like the Trident, the Rocket Three was a fast, competent bike, but by 1971 BSA was in financial trouble, recording a massive loss. The once mighty firm was swallowed up by the new Norton Villiers Triumph company, and the last batch of triples — wearing the well-known Triumph badges — left BSA's famous Small Heath factory in 1973.

■ BELOW *The ultimate BSA parallel twin is a genuine Rocket Gold Star such as this immaculate 1963 model.*

BUELL

■ BELOW *The heart of the Buell was Harley's 1200cc V-twin engine.*

■ BOTTOM *The RS1200 was a good Harley-powered sportsbike.*

■ BUELL RS1200

Harley-Davidson's reluctance to build a sportsbike in recent years has led many smaller firms and individuals to produce machines powered by the American firm's V-twin engine. Among those is Erik Buell, a former road-racer and Harley engineer, who designed and built an innovative, fully-faired bike called the RR1000, which was successful in twin-cylinder racing in the 1980s. The RR was followed in 1989 by the RS1200, a roadster whose half-fairing had the advantage of leaving the all important 1200cc Sportster V-twin unit in view.

The key to the Buell was its tubular steel frame, which held the engine via an ingenious rubber-mounting system.

BUELL RS1200 (1989)	
Engine	Aircooled 4-valve OHV pushrod 45-degree V-twin
Capacity	1200cc (88.8 x 96.8mm)
Power	70bhp @ 5000rpm
Weight	205kg (450lb) dry
Top speed	122mph (196kph)

Italian Marzocchi forks were matched with a rear shock set horizontally beneath the engine. The RS1200 roared to over 120mph (193kph) and handled well, but its high price kept sales low. Erik Buell's big break came in 1993, when Harley-Davidson – looking for a

way to diversify into the sportsbike market without spending a fortune on research and development or alienating its current riders – bought a 49 per cent stake in the firm, which was relaunched as the Buell Motorcycle Company.

In 1994, having moved into a newer and larger factory near Milwaukee, the new Buell firm launched its first bike: the S2 Thunderbolt. This too was powered by Harley's Sportster engine, and used a modified version of the RS frame. Reworked styling, new cycle parts and a free-breathing exhaust system made this the fastest and best Buell yet. Equally importantly, higher production levels allowed a lower price, and Buell now had input from Harley in development, finance and marketing. With plans for increased exports and a range of models including a roadster based on Harley's watercooled VR1000 race engine, the Buell Motorcycle Company looked set for an exciting future.

OTHER MAKES

■ BULTACO

Francisco Bulto founded Bultaco near Barcelona in 1958 after splitting from Montesa, which he had co-founded, due to that firm's reluctance to go racing. The new firm built a series of rapid small-

capacity two-stroke racers through the 1960s, and had many high finishes in Grands Prix. Roadsters included the rapid 250cc Metralla, which had a claimed top speed of more than 100mph (160kph). Bultaco also specialized in off-road bikes. Sammy Miller's win on a Sherpa in the 1965 Scottish Six Days Trial heralded the two-stroke's takeover in trials. After the trials world championship was started in 1975, Bultaco won five years in a row. In road racing, Angel Nieto and Ricardo Tormo won a total of four 50cc world titles in the years up to 1981. But by then a series of strikes had crippled Bultaco, and production ended shortly afterwards.

■ CABTON

One of several Japanese firms that built bikes heavily based on British singles and parallel twins in the 1950s, Cabton failed to survive the more competitive decade of the 1960s.

CAGIVA

■ CAGIVA C593

The last years were the best ones for Cagiva's 500cc Grand Prix challenge, as the Italian team that had dared take on the mighty Japanese factories in racing's toughest class finally won races in 1992 and 1993 – and saw John Kocinski briefly lead the 1994 500cc world championship on the bright red V-four. Then Cagiva quit Grands Prix, amid reports of financial problems for the group that owned Ducati, MV Agusta, Morini and Husqvarna as well as the Cagiva brand name.

Racing has always been the first love of Cagiva's owners, the Castiglioni brothers Claudio and Gianfranco, but the firm has produced some impressive roadsters since it was set up on the site of the former Aermacchi Harley-Davidson factory at Varese in 1978. Cagiva's rapid growth was based on 125cc two-strokes,

■ ABOVE *John Kocinski won the US Grand Prix in 1993, and briefly led the championship in 1994.*

most notable of which has been the race-replica Mito – a fine-handling 100mph (160kph) machine that has been regularly updated to provide cutting-edge style and performance.

Larger capacity Cagivas have included the 900 and 750cc Elefant trail bikes, derivatives of which have been successful in desert racing. The firm's withdrawal from Grands Prix in 1995 allowed more resources to be put into development of an exciting new range of 750 and 900cc four-cylinder machines destined for the street and World Superbike racetracks.

CAGIVA C593 (1993)

Engine	Watercooled 80-degree V-four crankcase reed-valve two-stroke
Capacity	498cc (56 x 50.6mm)
Power	178bhp @ 12,500rpm
Weight	132kg (290lb)
Top speed	191mph (306kph)

OTHER MAKES

■ CASAL

When Casal began production of its small-capacity two-strokes in the mid-1960s it relied on Zündapp engines. The Portuguese firm has since developed its own powerplants, and continues to build mainly 50cc bikes for the home market.

■ CCM

After building big-single motocross bikes based on BSA's B50 in the 1970s, British

specialist CCM was taken over by the Armstrong car components firm. Founder Alan Clews bought the company back in the mid-1980s and produced Rotax-engined motocross and trials bikes.

■ COTTON

Most of Cotton's production in the 1950s and 1960s consisted of modest roadsters with Villiers two-stroke engines. The firm had some racing history, though, and its "coTTon" badge was inspired by Stanley Woods' Isle of Man win in 1923.

■ CYCLONE

Famous for its exotic 1000cc, overhead-camshaft V-twins, Cyclone began to

build bikes in 1913 and won many races with them. But the American firm's roadsters were not profitable. Bigger firms, including Harley-Davidson and Indian, introduced eight-valve racers of their own, and Cyclone production lasted only for a few years.

■ CZ

Czech firm CZ began building bikes in the 1930s, and won several motocross world titles with its single-cylinder two-strokes in the 1960s. After the Second World War CZ was nationalized and produced utility roadsters in collaboration with Jawa, before Cagiva took control of the company in 1992.

■ LEFT *Cotton's Telstar racer of the mid-1960s used a 30bhp Villiers single-cylinder engine.*

■ BELOW LEFT *Trials star Dave Thorpe in action on a 250cc CCM in 1979.*

■ ABOVE *The 1994 version of Cagiva's 125cc Mito featured a 30bhp two-stroke engine, aluminium beam frame and styling inspired by Ducati's 916.*

■ OPPOSITE *Cagiva's V4 has generally been the most stylish, if not the fastest, of the factory 500s.*

■ RIGHT *Cagiva's Elefant 900 was a sophisticated trail bike powered by a Ducati V-twin engine.*

DOUGLAS

■ DOUGLAS DRAGONFLY

The flat-twin engine was Douglas's trademark, and the firm from Bristol concentrated on that layout from 1906 – when the Douglas family began building bikes previously known as Fairys – until its demise in the late 1950s. Early

DOUGLAS DRAGONFLY (1955)

Engine	Aircooled 4-valve OHV pushrod flat-twin
Capacity	348cc (60.8 x 60mm)
Power	17bhp @ 6000rpm
Weight	166kg (365lb)
Top speed	75mph (120kph)

models had boxer engines in line with the bike, including the banked sidecar outfit that versatile racing star Freddie Dixon used to win the 1923 sidecar TT. Roadsters such as the K32 were among the most sophisticated of the 1930s.

Later boxers such as the 350cc T35 of 1947 mounted the cylinders across the frame in BMW style, but although performance was good Douglas gained a reputation for dubious quality of both workmanship and materials. The last and best model was the 350cc Dragonfly, which was launched in 1955 and featured a headlamp nacelle that blended into the fuel tank. Aided by stout Earles forks and well-damped twin

rear shock units, the handling was excellent. But although the Dragonfly cruised smoothly and comfortably at 60mph (96kph), its low-rev performance and 75mph (120kph) top speed were moderate, and sales were not enough to keep Douglas in business.

■ ABOVE *The Dragonfly's 348cc flat-twin engine was not highly successful, lacking real smoothness at low revs.*

■ LEFT *Flowing styling and a Reynolds-Earles pivoted front fork gave the Dragonfly a distinctive look.*

■ RIGHT *Early Douglas twins, such as this 2.75bhp model from 1914, had cylinders in line with the bike.*

■ FAR RIGHT *Douglas introduced the disc brake on this 6bhp racebike in 1922.*

OTHER MAKES

■ DAIMLER

German engineer Gottlieb Daimler is credited with building the world's first motorcycle, the wooden-framed Einspur that was first ridden by his son Paul in 1885. Daimler had no great interest in motorcycles, and shortly afterwards abandoned the project to concentrate on automobile development.

■ DERBI

Barcelona firm Derbi's name showed its roots, DERivados de BIcicletus meaning "derivative of bicycles" – which is what they had built until the 250cc Super was released in 1950. Early motorcycles included a 350cc twin but in the 1960s Derbi concentrated on small-capacity bikes such as the racy 49cc and 74cc Grand Sports. The firm's successful challenge in Grand Prix racing's smaller classes culminated in Angel Nieto winning five 50cc and 125cc world titles between 1969 and 1972, when Derbi pulled out to concentrate on road bikes and motocross. Over a decade later the firm returned to Grands Prix to win a string of titles with another legendary Spanish rider, Jorge "Aspar" Martinez.

■ DKW

Founded by Danish-born Joerge Rasmussen, two-stroke specialist DKW began building bikes in 1920 and by 1928 had become the world's largest manufacturer with a production of over 100,000 machines. In 1932 DKW merged with Audi, Horsch and Wanderer to form Auto Union, giving the four-circle logo still

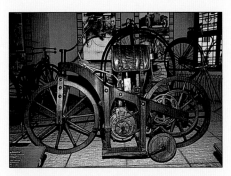

■ ABOVE *Daimler's 265cc Einspur had a top speed of about 8mph (12kph).*

■ ABOVE *Spanish stars and Derbi teammates Jorge Martinex and Alex Criville were closely matched at Jerez in 1988.*

■ ABOVE *The SB500 Luxus became the 300,000th DKW bike to be built when it rolled off the German firm's line in 1935.*

used by Audi. Numerous racing successes included Ewald Kluge's 1938 Junior TT win on a supercharged 250cc split-single. After the Second World War the Zschoppau factory was taken over by MZ, and DKW moved to Ingoldstadt in West Germany. In 1957 the firm joined the Victoria and Express companies in the Zweirad Union, but in 1966 this was bought by two-stroke engine manufacturer Fichtel & Sachs, who dropped the DKW name.

■ DMW

Wolverhampton-based DMW was founded during the Second World War to make suspension systems for rigid framed bikes, and progressed to building complete machines in 1947. Most were Villiers-engined two-strokes, notably the 250cc twin-cylinder Dolomite. Roadster production ended in 1966, although DMW continued to build trials bikes on a limited basis.

■ DNEPR

For many years Ukrainian firm Dnepr has built shaft-driven flat-twins based on BMW designs from the 1940s. The Dnepr 11 was a 649cc twin, producing 36bhp. Designed for use with a sidecar, it had a reverse gear and a top speed of about 75mph (120kph). The broadly similar military-style Dnepr 16 outfit featured drive to both rear wheels.

■ DOT

DOT's Lancashire factory built Villiers-engined trials and motocross two-strokes in the 1950s and 1960s. The firm's best decade was the 1920s, when DOT riders competed in the TT and its roadster range included a 1000cc JAP-powered V-twin.

DUCATI

■ DUCATI 250 DESMO

In 1926 the Ducati brothers, Adriano and Marcello, founded a company in Bologna to produce electrical components. Badly damaged in the Second World War, the factory was taken over by the government in exchange for their investment. Ducati looked for new opportunities, and in 1946 began producing the Cucciolo, a 50cc four-stroke engine that clipped onto a bicycle frame and sold in huge numbers. In 1954 the firm appointed a new chief designer, Fabio Taglioni, who would be responsible for many great bikes, and

DUCATI 250 DESMO (1975)	
Engine	Aircooled 2-valve SOHC desmodromic single
Capacity	249cc (74 x 57.8mm)
Power	30bhp @ 8000rpm
Weight	132kg (290lb) wet
Top speed	95mph (152kph)

for adopting the desmodromic system of valve operation – that is valves closed by a cam, rather than springs – that has become the company's trademark.

■ ABOVE
Taglioni's classical single, featured bevel shaft, single overhead cam and desmo valvegear.

■ LEFT *The 250 Desmo single's uncompromising approach was emphasized by its simple and elegant styling.*

■ ABOVE LEFT *Ducati's first engine was the 50cc Cucciolo, or "little pup", which clipped to a bicycle.*

■ ABOVE RIGHT *The 450cc desmo engine was also used to power a successful Street Scrambler model.*

■ ABOVE *The 100cc Grand Sport, Taglioni's first design for Ducati, set the tone for many future models.*

By 1955 Taglioni had produced the 100cc Grand Sport, known as the Marianna, whose single-cylinder engine, with overhead camshaft driven by bevel shaft, would provide Ducati's basic format for the next 20 years. The single was very successful in events like the Giro d'Italia, and in 1958 a 125cc desmo racebike won several Grands Prix and finished second in the world championship. Ducati's range grew with singles like the 175cc Sport of 1957, and the 1964 model 250cc Mach 1 – fast, light, stylish and successful on road and track.

The fastest and best singles of all were the Desmo roadsters, produced in 250, 350 and 450cc versions from the early 1970s. With sleek, simple styling by Leo Tartarini, they were sportsters with clip-on bars, rearset pegs and single seats. Both larger models were capable of over 100mph (160kph), and even the smallest Desmo came close, with reasonable smoothness and fine handling to match. Ducati also built a Street Scrambler version of the single, which sold well and was a predecessor of modern trail bikes.

■ RIGHT *Fine handling was always one of the light, firmly suspended Ducati singles' assets.*

![] DUCATI

■ DUCATI 900SS

Lean, loud and built purely for speed,
Ducati's 900SS was the most singleminded and arguably the finest of the
great Italian sportsters of the 1970s. The
900SS combined a potent V-twin engine

DUCATI 900SS (1975)

Engine	Aircooled 4-valve SOHC desmodromic 90-degree V-twin
Capacity	864cc (86 x 74.4mm)
Power	79bhp @ 7000rpm
Weight	188kg (414lb)
Top speed	132mph (211kph)

with a taut chassis, top-class cycle parts
and a racy riding position to provide
performance that few rivals could
approach. Its gaping, filterless 40mm
(1.5in) Dell'Orto carburettors, free-
breathing Conti pipes and lack of such
niceties as electric start or pillion seat,
left no doubt about its aggressive nature.

Ducati had released its first V-twin,
the 750GT, in 1971 and followed it
shortly afterwards with the tuned 750
Sport, an unfaired roadster with bright
yellow paintwork. Paul Smart's victory in
the 1972 Imola 200 inspired the
Bologna firm to build a street-legal
replica called the 750SS with desmodromic valve operation like the racer's.
In 1975 the engine was enlarged to

864cc to produce the 900SS, whose
maximum of 79bhp and generous mid-
range torque gave great acceleration and
a top speed of over 130mph (209kph).

The 900SS carried virtually no components that were not strictly necessary,

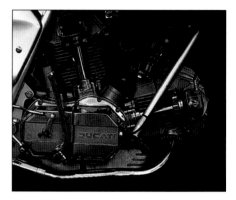

■ ABOVE *Big
Dell'Orto carbs
and thunderous
Conti pipes helped
the desmo V-twin
produce 79bhp.*

■ LEFT *The
original 900SS
was the most
singleminded of all
1970s superbikes –
a pure-bred racer
on the road.*

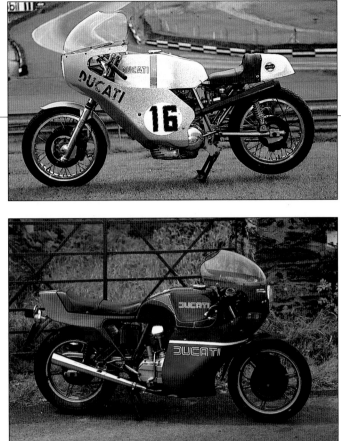

and the bike's light weight, strong
tubular steel frame and firm Marzocchi
suspension parts gave unshakeable
high-speed handling. A useful cockpit
fairing, Brembo brakes and elegant
styling added to the charm of a bike that
could be raced successfully in production events with few modifications.

Ducati's success in the 1970s owed
much to two racing victories, both by
Englishmen but in very different
circumstances. Paul Smart's unexpected
win at the prestigious Imola 200 in April
1972 was a landmark. Smart finished
just ahead of team-mate Bruno
Spaggiari, beating several factory entries
including MV Agusta's Giacomo
Agostini, for a result that did much to
establish the Ducati name worldwide.

Six years later came another famous
day, when Mike Hailwood returned from
retirement to win the Isle of Man
Formula One TT. Hailwood's emotional
victory on the red and green Sports
Motorcycles V-twin, at an average speed
of 108.51mph (174.6 kph), led to
Ducati producing a limited edition

Hailwood Replica of the 900SS in 1979.
Like the standard 900, it remained in
production until 1984, steadily losing its
performance edge due to tightening
emissions laws and Ducati's growing
financial problems, which led to the
state-owned firm being taken over by
Cagiva in 1985.

■ TOP *Paul Smart's legendary victory at
the Imola 200 in 1972 gave the reputation
of Ducati's V-twins a big boost.*

■ ABOVE *Ducati celebrated Mike the
Bike's 1978 TT win with a successful
Hailwood Replica V-twin.*

■ BELOW *The 750 Sport of the early
1970s featured a 56bhp V-twin engine.*

43

DUCATI

■ DUCATI 916

Rarely has a new motorcycle generated as much excitement as Ducati's 916 did on its launch in 1994. The bike's styling was feline and gorgeous, from the sleek scarlet nose of its twin-headlamp fairing, via a single-sided swing-arm, to the tailpiece from which emerged twin high-level silencers. Its fuel-injected V-twin engine was magnificent, churning out mid-range torque and a peak of 114bhp. And its chassis was sublime, combining state-of-the-art suspension technology with the strength and simplicity of Ducati's traditional tubular steel frame.

The 916, designed by a team headed by former Bimota co-founder Massimo Tamburini, was the ultimate development of the watercooled, eight-valve desmodromic V-twin series that had begun with Massimo Bordi's 851 Strada in 1988. The 851 had brought Ducati, revitalized under Cagiva's control, roaring into the 1990s, combining the V-twin's traditional torque and charm with a new-found refinement. Over the next few years the Bologna firm's flagship was reshaped, its chassis was revised and its engine was enlarged to 888cc, giving additional speed and poise.

The 916 raised the stakes again, with a top speed of 160mph (257kph), even more mid-range acceleration and the addictive feel that only a V-twin can provide. Its uprated chassis gave light steering with impeccable stability, plus

DUCATI 916 (1994)	
Engine	Watercooled 8-valve DOHC desmodromic 90-degree V-twin
Capacity	916cc (94 x 66mm)
Power	114bhp @ 9000rpm
Weight	195kg (429lb)
Top speed	160mph (257kph)

■ BELOW *The 916 was beautiful, from its sharp nose to its high-level silencers.*

■ BELOW *In 1990 French ace Raymond Roche began Ducati's world Superbike domination.*

■ RIGHT *The sophisticated eight-valve 851 (left) was joined by the simpler, four-valve 900SS in 1989.*

huge amounts of cornering clearance and grip. Parent company Cagiva's financial problems resulted in delayed production, increasing the demand for what had already been the most eagerly awaited new bike for years. Everyone who finally got to ride the 916 knew that this was a very special motorcycle.

Much of Ducati's sales success in the 1990s was due to domination of the World Superbike Championship, in which the Italian firm benefited from rules allowing twin-cylinder bikes a capacity and weight advantage over fours. Frenchman Raymond Roche won the title in 1990, and American Doug Polen followed with successive championships on the factory V-twins. After coming second to Kawasaki's Scott Russell in 1993, Britain's Carl Fogarty gained revenge with victory on his works 916 the following season.

Ducati also developed a fine line of less high-tech V-twins, after reviving the 900SS name for a new SOHC, two-valves-per-cylinder desmo sportster in 1989. That red and white model suffered from mediocre carburation and suspension, but two years later it was

uprated and reshaped to produce a thrillingly raw superbike. In the following years the 900SS line was broadened to include the single-seat Superlight and the stylish, unfaired M900 Monster, plus lookalike Super Sport models in 750 and 600cc sizes.

■ ABOVE AND INSET LEFT *The M900 Monster's brutal styling and wheelie-happy performance made it a big hit.*

ENFIELD

■ ENFIELD BULLET 500

The single-cylinder Bullet was one of the most popular models of Britain's old Royal Enfield firm, which manufactured the simple, light bike between 1949 and 1962, initially in 350cc and later in 500cc form. The Bullet was widely exported, and was used by the Indian armed forces. In 1958 production was started in Madras, using machinery from the old Royal Enfield factory. The 350cc bike sold well in India, and by the mid-1980s it was also being exported to

much-improved front brake. By modern standards the Enfield was inevitably crude, with modest acceleration, a realistic cruising speed of 65mph (104kph), considerable vibration and harsh handling. It was also cheap, economical, reliable and provided an unmistakable classic feel that some riders enjoyed.

ENFIELD BULLET 500 (1990)

Engine	Aircooled 2-valve OHV pushrod single
Capacity	499cc (84 x 90mm)
Power	22bhp @ 5400rpm
Weight	169kg (270lb)
Top speed	80mph (128kph)

countries including Britain.

The 500cc model followed a few years later and was also successful, despite its basic layout having remained unchanged since the mid-1950s. The pushrod-operated engine produced 22bhp, and was held in a simple tubular steel frame. For domestic use many of the details had changed little, too, but export bikes incorporated numerous refinements including a

■ BELOW *The 500cc Bullet was built in 1990 but looks almost identical to its predecessor of the 1950s.*

■ RIGHT *Bullet handling is inevitably crude but can be uprated by specialists such as Fritz Egli.*

■ OPPOSITE MIDDLE *Even when tuned the pushrod Bullet engine lacks power, but it is economical and fairly reliable.*

OTHER MAKES

■ ECOMOBILE

Looking like a large, wingless glider, the Ecomobile produced by Swiss engineer Arnold Wagner was one of the most unusual machines on two wheels. The first versions, produced in 1982, held a BMW flat-twin engine in the Kevlar/fibreglass monocoque body. In 1988 the design was uprated using the four-cylinder K100 engine, giving the streamlined Ecomobile a top speed of over 150mph (241kph).

■ EGLI

Swiss engineer Fritz Egli has built chassis, invariably featuring his trademark large-diameter steel spine frame, for a huge variety of engines since starting with the Vincent V-twin on which he became Swiss racing champion in the late 1960s. In the 1970s he turned to four-cylinder Hondas and Kawasakis, and his bikes were highly successful in endurance racing. In recent years he has produced his first Harley-Davidson special. And as the Swiss and Austrian importer of Enfield Bullets, he tuned the Indian-made single's engine and

■ ABOVE *Egli's 1983 Harley special, nicknamed Lucifer's Hammer, was fast, loud and powerful.*

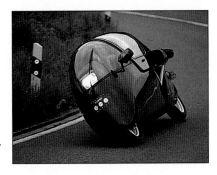

uprated its chassis to produce the considerably improved Swiss Finish Bullet.

■ ELF

The string of racebikes backed by French petrochemicals giant Elf were some of the most innovative of recent years, all using non-telescopic suspension of various designs. Radical early models such as the Honda-powered Elf E endurance racer of 1981 pioneered features including carbon fibre disc brakes. In 1985 Elf moved into Grands Prix with backing from Honda, using a more conventional forkless chassis. Despite a works V-four engine, British rider Ron Haslam could never make the Elf 3 truly competitive, and Elf pulled out after the 1988 season. Honda's involvement yielded benefits including development of the single-sided swing-arm found on many recent roadsters.

■ EMC

Austrian-born two-stroke tuning wizard Dr Joe Ehrlich came to England in the 1930s and set up his Ehrlich Motor Co in London after the War. His Model S and Model T 350s used unusual split-single engines, and were unsuccessful. In the early 1960s

■ LEFT *The amazing 170mph (273kph) Turbo Ecomobile combined superbike speed and cornering ability with sports car comfort.*

■ ABOVE *Ron Haslam lifts the Elf 3's forkless front wheel at the 1988 French Grand Prix.*

Ehrlich built a 125cc racer on which Mike Hailwood scored good results. After a successful move to F3 car racing Ehrlich returned to bikes in the early 1980s, when his 250cc Rotax-engined racers were highly competitive in Grands Prix and the TT. After another absence, the veteran Dr Joe – now in his 80s – returned with yet another EMC racebike in 1995.

EXCELSIOR

■ EXCELSIOR MANXMAN

Excelsior became Britain's first motorcycle manufacturer when it began selling
bikes in 1896 under the firm's original
name of Bayliss, Thomas and Co. In

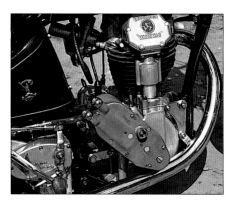

1910 the company's name was changed
to Excelsior, following the demise of a
German manufacturer of the same name.
Excelsior specialized in small-capacity
bikes and produced racers, notably the

250cc Mechanical Marvel – which won
the Lightweight TT in 1933.

That result increased interest in
Excelsior and led to the firm producing
a replica racer, but a loss of nerve by the

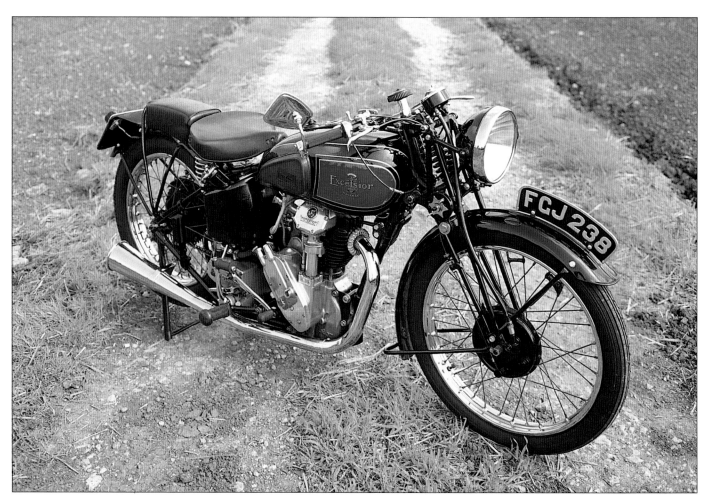

EXCELSIOR MANXMAN 250 (1936)

Engine	Aircooled 2-valve SOHC single
Capacity	246cc (63 x 79mm)
Power	25bhp approx
Weight	132kg (290lb) dry
Top speed	80mph (128kph)

OTHER MAKES

■ EXCELSIOR

The American motorcycles of this name were built in Chicago by the Schwinn bicycle company, and ranged from small two-strokes to the big four-stroke V-twins for which Excelsior was famous. The firm built its first machine in 1907. By 1931, when Excelsior fell victim to the Depression, the factory had taken over production of the four-cylinder Henderson, becoming America's third largest marque behind Indian and Harley-Davidson. Excelsior's best known model was the Super X, a 750cc (45ci) V-twin introduced in the mid-1920s.

engineers – who thought club racers would be unable to maintain such a complicated engine – prompted a simpler motor with a single overhead camshaft. The Manxman was released in 1935 in 250cc form, and was later produced in 350 and 500cc capacities too. Its good performance and impressive strength made the single popular with road riders and club racers.

After the Second World War, Excelsior concentrated on Villiers-engined two-stroke roadsters such as the 250cc Viking and Talisman, but sales fell and production came to an end in 1962.

■ OPPOSITE TOP
A Manxman at speed on the TT circuit from which its name is derived.

■ OPPOSITE
MIDDLE *The Excelsior's SOHC engine, seen here in 350cc form, was simple and reliable.*

■ OPPOSITE
BELOW *As well as being a competitive racer, the Manxman was a popular roadster in the late 1930s.*

■ RIGHT
Excelsior's 250cc four-valve Mechanical Marvel was ridden to TT victory by Sid Gleave in 1933.

FN

■ BELOW AND BOTTOM *In 1911, few bikes could even approach the sophistication of the FN's four-cylinder engine and shaft final drive.*

■ FN FOUR

The world's first mass-produced four-cylinder motorcycle was the Belgian-built FN, which was a revelation when it was introduced in 1904. The company had been founded near Liège in 1899 to manufacture arms and ammunition, and began making single-cylinder bikes in 1902. But it is the four-cylinder bike, designed by Paul Kelecom, for which FN is remembered. The 362cc in-line engine was notable for its high tension magneto ignition and fully-enclosed shaft final drive; the chassis incorporated one of the earliest forms of telescopic forks.

Initial doubts led *France Automobile* magazine to regard it as more of a curiosity than a practical motorcycle,

FN FOUR (1911)

Engine	Aircooled 8-valve inlet-over-exhaust in-line four
Capacity	491cc
Power	4bhp
Weight	75kg (165lb) dry
Top speed	40mph (64kph)

despite its remarkable engine. But the FN was far more than that, and would be gradually updated over two decades of production. Engine capacity grew to 412cc and then to 491cc in 1911, by which time the FN Four produced about 4hp, had gained a clutch and two-speed gearbox, and was capable of 40mph. An

updated 748cc four was introduced just before the First World War during which the occupied factory produced bikes for the German army. The FN did not recapture its popularity after the War, although a 1923 redesign – when chain final drive replaced the shaft – kept the model going for three more years.

OTHER MAKES

■ FANTIC

After starting production in the 1960s, Fantic gained a reputation for small-capacity two-strokes, particularly the range of Caballero trail bikes. The Italian firm has built many bikes for motocross and particularly trials, where it has been a leading contender for many years.

■ FATH

German racer-engineer Helmut Fath's greatest achievement came not in 1960, when he won the world sidecar championship for the first time, but eight years later, when he returned from serious injury to regain the title on a machine he had designed and built himself. The URS, named after Fath's village of Ursenbach, was a 500cc DOHC transverse four that revved to 15,000rpm and produced a reported 80bhp. The URS was also raced as a solo using chassis from Seeley and Metisse, most successfully in 1969 by veteran German Karl Hoppe. After selling his team to Friedel Münch, Fath built a powerful 500cc flat-four two-stroke engine that was raced in both solo and sidecar classes in the 1970s.

■ FRANCIS-BARNETT

Never the most glamorous of manufacturers, Francis-Barnett specialized in producing economical roadsters from its start in 1919 until its demise in 1966. The firm's most famous model was the 250 Cruiser of the 1930s, which combined its single-cylinder Villiers two-stroke engine with pressed-steel leg-shields, large mud-guards and partial engine covers. In 1947, the Coventry firm was taken over by Associated Motor Cycles, after which it continued to build small-capacity roadsters, as well as trials and scrambles bikes, profitably for several years. But the rise of Italian scooters hit sales, and Francis-Barnett's attempt to design and build its own engines was unsuccessful. "Fanny-B" returned to Villiers engines for its single and twin-cylinder models, also called Cruisers, in the 1960s.

■ RIGHT *This single-cylinder Francis-Barnett Falcon provided reasonable small-capacity performance in 1959.*

■ LEFT *Helmut Fath won the 1968 sidecar world title with his own four-cylinder URS.*

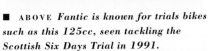
■ ABOVE *The bodywork of this 1936-model Francis-Barnett Cruiser gave its rider useful protection.*

■ ABOVE *Fantic is known for trials bikes such as this 125cc, seen tackling the Scottish Six Days Trial in 1991.*

GILERA

■ GILERA SATURNO

Gilera was one of motorcycling's big names in the 1950s, racing with great success and building some fine roadsters. The firm was founded by a youthful Giuseppe Gilera in 1909, and represented Italy in the International Six Days Trial in the 1930s. Gilera's most famous roadsters were four-stroke singles, notably the 500cc Saturno that was much loved for its blend of clean, handsome styling and lively performance.

The Saturno was designed and briefly raced just before Italy entered the Second World War but was first produced in 1946, in Sport, Touring and Competition versions. Early models had girder forks and Gilera's own brand of rear suspension – horizontal springs in tubes, with friction dampers. Telescopic forks and vertical shocks were introduced in the early 1950s. The bike quickly became popular thanks to its

■ ABOVE *In recent years, the once-proud Gilera name has only been used for Piaggio-built scooters.*

GILERA SATURNO (1951)	
Engine	Aircooled 2-valve OHV pushrod single
Capacity	499cc (84 x 90mm)
Power	22bhp @ 5000rpm (Sport version)
Weight	170kg (374lb) dry
Top speed	85mph (136kph)

■ LEFT *The Saturno racer's look and performance changed little throughout most of the 1950s.*

■ OPPOSITE
The modern Saturno was a sporty roadster with traditional red finish and single-cylinder engine.

■ LEFT *The CX125, a two-stroke sportster introduced in 1991, featured single-sided suspension at front and rear.*

excellent road-going performance and some impressive racing results, notably Carlo Bandirola's win at the new Sanremo circuit in 1947, which led to the Saturno racer being known as the Sanremo.

Saturnos were not competitive at Grand Prix level but continued to be raced successfully in Italy several years after production had ended in the late 1950s. But by then Giuseppe Gilera had lost enthusiasm following the early death, of a heart attack, of his son Feruccio in 1956.

In 1969 the company was sold to small-bike specialist and Vespa scooter producer Piaggio, who developed a range of new models in the late 1980s. These included a new Saturno, a stylish 500cc four-stroke single with half-fairing, disc brakes and single-shock rear suspension, which was produced mainly for export to Japan. Later models included the Nordwest 600 single and

the CX125, an innovative two-stroke sportster with forkless front suspension. Sales, however, were moderate, and Gilera's 250cc Grand Prix comeback in 1992 was sadly an expensive failure

that the company could ill-afford. In 1993 Piaggio announced the closure of the factory at Arcore, near Milan, although the Gilera name continued to be used for scooters.

OTHER MAKES

■ GARELLI
When Garelli began production in 1913 it was with an unusual 350cc twin-pistoned two-stroke single, which won many races. Recent production has concentrated on

■ LEFT *Angel Nieto cornering his 125cc works Garelli.*

■ FAR LEFT
Spain's trials superstar Jordi Tarrés takes a rare "dab" to steady his factory Gas-Gas.

small-capacity two-strokes and mopeds. Garelli's most successful racing years were the 1980s, when the Italian firm's monocoque-framed 125cc parallel twins, acquired from Minarelli, won seven consecutive world titles at the hands of Fausto Gresini, Luca Cadalora and Angel Nieto.

■ GAS-GAS
Spanish specialist firm Gas-Gas has made a huge impact in trials over recent years, scoring numerous wins through their riders, including the great Jordi Tarrés who clinched his seventh world championship in 1995.

GILERA

■ GILERA 500cc FOUR

Gilera's 500cc four-cylinder racer made even more of an impact than its impressive haul of six world championships between 1950 and 1957 suggests. Its transverse four-engine layout provided the inspiration not only for MV Agusta, whose similar machines dominated the 500cc world championship after Gilera's withdrawal, but later also for the Japanese factories on both road and track.

The original 500 four was designed as early as 1923 by Carlo Gianini and Piero Remor, two young engineers from Rome. Initially aircooled and with a gear-driven single overhead camshaft, by 1934 the four was called the Rondine, featured twin cams and a

supercharger, and was producing an impressive 86bhp. Gilera bought the project, and the four was soon winning races and setting a world speed record of 170.15mph (273.8kph).

After the War supercharging was banned, halving the four's power output. Piero Remor, one of the original designers, produced a new aircooled, twin-cam powerplant, then in 1949 left for MV, who soon adopted a similar layout. Nevertheless Gilera's Umberto Masetti won two championships and Geoff Duke added three more between 1953 and 1955. After Libero Liberati's win in 1957 the Arcore firm joined rivals Guzzi and Mondial in pulling out of Grand Prix racing completely.

GILERA 500cc-FOUR (1956)

Engine	Aircooled 8-valve DOHC transverse four
Capacity	499cc (52 x 58.8mm)
Power	70bhp @ 11,000rpm
Weight	150kg (330lb) dry
Top speed	145mph (233kph)

■ RIGHT *John Hartle howls his Gilera through Quarter Bridge on the way to second place in the 1963 Senior TT.*

OTHER MAKES

GNOME & RHÔNE

Between the Wars the Paris-based factory moved from aircraft engine production to build a variety of bikes with single-cylinder and flat-twin engines of up to 750cc. After 1945 Gnome & Rhône built small-capacity two-strokes, but didn't survive the 1950s.

GREEVES

Best known for its trials and motocross bikes, Essex firm Greeves also built roadsters and the Silverstone road-racer in the 1950s and 1960s. Most of the roadsters were 250 and 350cc two-strokes, with engines bought from British Anzani or Villiers, and given names such as Fleetmaster, Sportsman and Sports Twin. Off-road successes included many wins for the

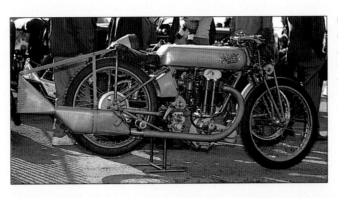

Greeves Hawkstone scrambler, and the European 250cc championships won by Dave Bickers in 1960 and 1961. Bill Wilkinson's Scottish Six Days Trial victory on a 250cc Greeves Anglian in 1969, ahead of Sammy Miller's Bultaco, brought to an end British bikes' domination of the trials world.

■ LEFT *The exhaust of this Grindlay-Peerless racer from the 1920s is fitted with a huge "Brooklands can" to reduce noise.*

GRINDLAY-PEERLESS

Bill Lacey gave Grindlay-Peerless its greatest success when he covered over 100 miles (160km) in an hour to set a world record in 1928. Roadsters ranged from big 1000cc V-twins to 150cc two-strokes, but although the bikes were regarded as stylish, production ended in 1934.

■ LEFT *This 250cc Sports Twin two-stroke from 1963 was typical of Greeves' roadster production.*

■ LEFT *Bill Wilkinson won the 1969 Scottish Six Days Trial on a 250cc, Villiers-engined works Greeves Anglian.*

HARLEY-DAVIDSON

■ BELOW *Harley's Model 9E of 1913 featured the 45-degree, V-twin engine layout that remains today.*

■ HARLEY-DAVIDSON MODEL 9E

William S Harley and Arthur Davidson were former school friends who, while working for a Milwaukee engineering firm, dreamt of producing a motorbike. In 1902 they built a 400cc (25ci) single-cylinder engine, and a year later, after being joined by Davidson's elder brothers Walter and William A, they fitted it into a bicycle frame to complete the prototype Harley-Davidson motorcycle. The motor proved reliable but underpowered, so was enlarged. The frame was too weak so it was replaced with a more substantial structure built along similar lines.

HARLEY-DAVIDSON MODEL 9E (1913)

Engine	Aircooled 2-valve inlet-over-exhaust single V-twin
Capacity	1000cc (61ci)
Power	10bhp
Weight	150kg (330lb) dry
Top speed	60mph (96kph)

Two more bikes were produced in 1903, and another three the following year. By 1907 the Harley-Davidson's growing reputation for reliability had helped push annual production above 150. In that year Harley-Davidson raised money for expansion by becoming a corporation, with shares divided among 17 employees. The firm had by now moved across Milwaukee from its first base, a small shed in the Davidsons' yard, to bigger premises in what would become Juneau Avenue, the firm's current address.

Very early models had no lights or suspension but within a few years Harley had fitted leading-link forks, a carbide gas headlamp and magneto ignition. The Model 5 of 1909 produced about 4bhp from its 494cc (30ci) inlet-over-exhaust engine, and was good for 45mph (72kph). It had bicycle pedals to

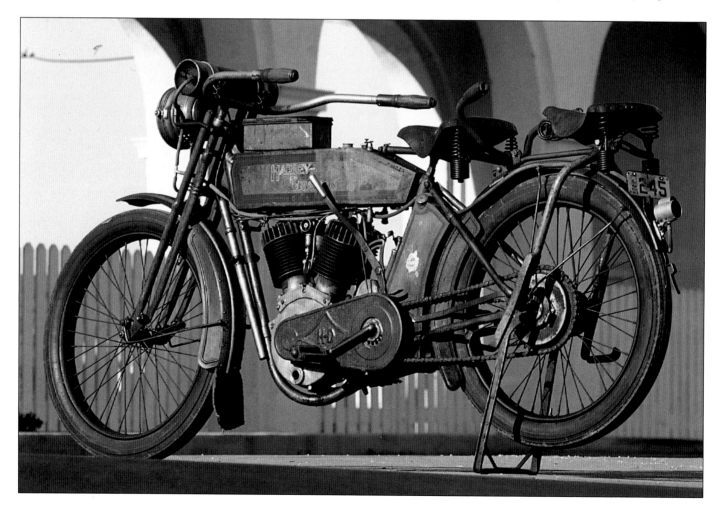

■ RIGHT *Harley made a late start in racing, but tuned and lightened V-twins such as this were successful after 1914.*

start the engine and set the bike in motion, after which the leather drive belt was tightened using a hand lever.

Harley's first V-twin, the Model 5D, was built in 1909, but was not an immediate success. It produced about 7bhp, almost twice as much as the

■ FAR LEFT *This official photograph from 1910 shows founders William, Walter and Arthur Davidson and William Harley.*

■ LEFT *The Harley legend began in this tiny shed at the rear of the Davidsons' home in Milwaukee.*

■ BELOW *Harley launched a new 5bhp single in 1913, and a year later introduced a kickstart and rear drum brake.*

single, but was hard to start and suffered from a slipping drive belt. Two years later the 45-degree V-twin was reintroduced with revised valvegear and a new frame; soon afterwards it was fitted with chain drive and a full floating seat. The improvements made a big difference and the V-twin grew rapidly in popularity. By 1913, the Model 9E's 1000cc (61ci) powerplant was producing about 10bhp, giving a top speed of 60mph (96kph).

Harley-Davidson had initially been reluctant to get involved in racing, preferring reliability runs, but in 1914 finally entered a factory team. The Milwaukee firm's so-called "Wrecking Crew", riding powerful eight-valve V-twins, were very competitive against rivals Indian, Merkel and Excelsior both before and after the First World War. This period was one of great fluctuation for Harley-Davidson. Production rose to over 22,000 bikes and 16,000 sidecars in 1919, before halving two years later due mainly to the rise of the Model T Ford, which put most of the American motorcycle firms out of business.

HARLEY-DAVIDSON

■ OPPOSITE *A neat pair of V-twins on show at Harley riders' unofficial meeting place at Daytona Beach, Florida.*

■ HARLEY-DAVIDSON WL45

Harley is best known for large-capacity V-twins, but the smaller 45ci (750cc) Forty Five also played a vital part in the company's history. The first 45ci model, a basic machine with a total-loss oil system, was produced in 1928. Nine

HARLEY WL45 (1949)

Engine	Aircooled sidevalve 45-degree V-twin
Capacity	742cc (70 x 97mm)
Power	25bhp @ 4000rpm
Weight	240kg (528lb) wet
Top speed	75mph (120kph)

■ BELOW *The look of this "hard-tail" 1949 WL45 is reflected in the styling of many modern Harleys.*

years later, it was restyled and updated to create the W series. Simple and strong, if not particularly fast even in its day, the Forty Five kept Harley going through the Depression of the 1930s. As the WLA model it also proved an ideal military machine, with around 80,000 being used in the Second World War.

After the War many ex-army 45s were converted for civilian use, which did much to popularize Harleys worldwide, and the Milwaukee factory recommenced building the W in various forms, including the WR racer. The WL name denoted a sportier version of the basic W, with slightly raised compression increasing power to 25bhp. The three-speed gearbox was operated by a hand lever, with a foot clutch. In 1949 Harley introduced its Girdraulic damping system on the WL's springer front forks,

■ ABOVE *The K-series V-twin, introduced in 1952, featured unit construction and a four-speed gearbox.*

in place of the simple friction damper used previously. The bike had a sprung saddle and no rear suspension.

Nevertheless the ride was fairly comfortable, handling was adequate and the WL was capable of cruising steadily and reliably at 60mph (96kph). It remained in production until 1952, when it was replaced by the Model K,

featuring a unit-construction engine and four-speed gearbox, with foot change. The three-wheeled Servicar, powered by the faithful 45ci engine, was built until 1974.

In 1936, with America still suffering the effects of the Depression, Harley bravely introduced the Model 61E. The new bike's 61ci (1000cc) V-twin engine

was a major advance due to its over-head-valve design and recirculating oil system. The 61E was also neatly styled, and became a big success. Known as the Knucklehead after the shape of the engine's rocker covers, it gave Harley the technical edge over great rivals Indian and became the illustrious ancestor of all modern Harleys.

■ RIGHT *The shape of this 1946 Knucklehead's rocker covers clearly shows where it got its name from.*

■ ABOVE *Harley's wartime WLA and WLC, built for Canadian forces, proved to be rugged and reliable.*

■ ABOVE *The three-wheeled Servicar, produced for commercial use in 1931, was a long-running success.*

HARLEY-DAVIDSON

■ HARLEY-DAVIDSON XLCH SPORTSTER

At its peak in the early 1960s, the XLCH Sportster lived up to its name by being one of the quickest bikes on the road. It roared to a top speed of over 100mph (160kph), turned standing quarters in around 14 seconds and, in a straight line at least, was a match for lighter British 650cc twins. That was then. In recent decades the name has remained while the Sportster models, smallest machines in a range of cruisers, have become about as far from a sports motorcycle as possible.

The Sportster was launched in 1957, with an overhead valve V-twin motor

HARLEY-DAVIDSON XLCH SPORTSTER (1962)

Engine	Aircooled 4-valve OHV pushrod 45-degree V-twin
Capacity	883cc (76.2 x 96.8mm)
Power	55bhp @ 5000rpm
Weight	220kg (485lb)
Top speed	110mph (177kph)

■ LEFT *The original XLCH's 883cc engine-capacity is also used for the smaller of the two current Sportster models.*

■ BELOW *Lean, loud, powerful and respectably light, the Sportster fully lived up to its name back in 1959.*

■ LEFT *By 1991, the Sportster's capacity had grown to 1200cc but its performance had barely changed at all.*

■ BELOW *Harley attempted to build a true sportsbike with the XLCR Café Racer of 1977, but it was not a great success.*

for mediocre suspension and brakes by plenty of others, the current XLHs are the best yet, combining age-old charm with five-speed gearboxes, belt final drive systems and reliability unheard of from Milwaukee in 1957. Its name may not ring true any more, but the Sportster looks set to stick around for many more years to come.

In contrast, one of Harley's most distinctive but least successful, and shortest-lived, models of all was the lean black XLCR Café Racer that was introduced in 1977. Consisting of the 1000cc Sportster engine in a new frame developed from that of the XR750 racebike, the Café Racer incorporated racy features such as a bikini fairing, twin front discs, matt-black siamesed exhausts and single seat. The look was attractive and by Harley standards the performance was good, but the XLCR appealed neither to traditional riders nor to the café racer crowd. Few were sold and the model was quickly dropped; ironically it has become quite highly sought-after in recent years.

whose 54ci (883cc) capacity was the same as its KH predecessor, but used a larger bore and shorter stroke to allow higher revs. The original XL model had a big gas tank and fenders, but a year later Harley produced the XLCH, complete with tuned engine, small headlamp, tiny gas tank, lower bars and loud pipes: the classical Sportster style had arrived.

The Sportster's look and performance have varied remarkably little over the years. Capacity has increased via 1000cc to 1200cc, joined in 1986 by the Evolution-engined 883cc model that has served as a popular entry-level Harley. Although frequently derided by riders of big-twin Harleys, and criticized

HARLEY-DAVIDSON

■ HARLEY-DAVIDSON ELECTRA GLIDE

For many people the Electra Glide is the quintessential Harley-Davidson: big, simple, traditional, ostentatious; a bike built by Americans, for Americans, for travelling across the vast country of its birth. More than just a comfortable, slow-revving V-twin tourer, the Electra Glide has become a rumbling, rolling symbol of two-wheeled freedom – albeit one hampered over the years by dubious reliability, handling and braking.

The Electra Glide was launched in 1965, when Harley added an electric starter to the 74ci (1200cc) V-twin that had been steadily developed since

1947. The legendary name followed a pattern; the 1949 model Hydra-Glide featured hydraulic front suspension and the Duo-Glide of 1958 had added rear

■ LEFT *Harley introduced fuel-injection with the range-topping Ultra Classic Electra Glide in 1995.*

■ BELOW *This 1978 Glide shows classic features, including big fenders, fat tyres and lots of chrome.*

suspension. With high handlebars, big gas tank and fenders, footboards, a single saddle, and fat white-wall tyres on wire-spoked wheels, the Electra

■ LEFT *The Hydra-Glide was introduced in 1949, taking its name from its new hydraulic front forks.*

to benefit from the hugely improved alloy Evolution engine introduced by a revitalized Harley in 1984 – from which point it has been success all the way. In 1995, the range-topping Ultra Classic Electra Glide debuted the fuel-injection system designed to take Harley's faithful aircooled, pushrod V-twin towards the 21st century.

The Electra Glide may have been the most famous Harley, but the Softail model introduced in 1984 was perhaps the most significant. As well as the new Evolution engine, the Softail featured clean, traditional looks and rear suspension cleverly hidden under the engine to give the illusion of a solid or "hard-tail" rear end.

The Softail marked Harley's entry into the nostalgia market that has served the company so well ever since. Its most vivid interpretation came in 1993 with the Heritage Softail Nostalgia – complete with two-tone paint, white-wall tyres and cowhide patches on both the seat and the saddlebags.

HARLEY-DAVIDSON ELECTRA GLIDE (1965)

Engine	Aircooled 4-valve OHV pushrod 45-degree V-twin
Capacity	1198cc (87.1 x 100.6mm)
Power	60bhp @ 4000rpm
Weight	350kg (770lb)
Top speed	95mph (152kph)

■ ABOVE *Styling chief Willie G Davidson, grandson of William A, has played a big part in Harley's recent success.*

■ BELOW *The Heritage Softail Nostalgia sums up Harley's approach to design.*

Glide looked elegant. Despite plenty of engine vibration and poor suspension and braking – problems exaggerated by its massive 350kg of weight – the bike was well received.

Just a year later, in 1966, Harley changed the engine from the Panhead to the Shovelhead – named after the shape of their cylinder head covers – which added a modicum of reliability. Other changes over the years included adding a fairing and hard luggage, enlarging the V-twin lump to 80ci (1340cc) in 1978, and rubber-mounting the powerplant to combat vibration. All helped make the Glide ride better and in more comfort.

The biggest shake-up in Harley-Davidson history came in 1981 when the management, led by Vaughn Beals, raised the money to buy Harley from parent company AMF, under whose control in the 1970s Harley had seen a deterioration in quality and sales. The Electra Glide was one of the first models

■ BELOW *Harley's XR750 engine features big cooling fins, extra-strong cases and gearshift on the right side.*

■ BOTTOM *The lean purposeful look of the XR is partially ruined by the massive muffler on the left side.*

HARLEY-DAVIDSON

■ HARLEY-DAVIDSON XR750

One bike has dominated American dirt-track racing since the early 1970s: Harley's XR750, the thundering V-twin that has captured countless victories

HARLEY-DAVIDSON XR750 (1978)

Engine	Aircooled 4-valve pushrod OHV 45-degree V-twin
Capacity	750cc (79 x 76mm)
Power	95bhp @ 8000rpm
Weight	145kg (319lb) wet
Top speed	130mph (209kph)

while retaining almost the same look and layout. The XR was introduced in 1970, when race-team manager Dick O'Brien put a modified Sportster engine into the chassis of Harley's outdated KR racer. The result was initially underpowered, unreliable and unsuccessful; the original XR's best performances were arguably made by car-jumping stunt rider Evel Knievel. But in 1972 the XR's iron-barrelled engine was replaced by a new aluminium V-twin, and Mark Brelsford won the first of its many titles.

The Harley has not always been on top since then. Yamaha's Kenny Roberts won in 1973 and 1974, and in the mid-1980s Honda won four titles with the

RS750, which was based on a CX500 V-twin engine turned through 90 degrees. But the XR750 has generally ruled the roost, with championships for riders including Jay Springsteen, who won three in a row from 1976-8, and Randy

■ LEFT *Rodney Ferris crouches low and revs his Harley XR750 towards 130mph (209kph) at the Sacramento Mile.*

■ FAR LEFT TOP *Scott Parker and his factory XR have been successful in recent seasons.*

■ FAR LEFT BOTTOM *Italian star Walter Villa won four 250 and 350cc world titles in the mid-1970s.*

■ BELOW *Harley revealed a new generation of V-twin technology in the alloy-framed V1000 racebike.*

Goss, a double champion in the early 1980s. Most successful of all has been Scott Parker, who in 1994 clinched his fifth national championship and record 60th race win – all on the XR750.

Since 1980, Harley has not built complete XRs, instead selling engines which are then built into bikes using parts from firms such as frame specialist Champion. A modern XR750 produces over 100bhp, and reaches over 130mph (209kph). In over 30 years the lean and purposeful XR look has barely changed, despite the appearance of upside-down forks, cast wheels, rear brakes – early XRs had none at all – and huge silencers. Many road machines have copied its style, including Harley's own 1983 model XR1000, and Sportster-based XR specials from firms such as Storz Performance and Los Angeles dealer Bartels.

The XR750 has never made as good a road racer as it has a dirt-track bike, but the Harley has had its moments over the years. Some of its best performances came from Cal Rayborn at the Anglo-American match race series in 1972. The Californian won three races and set

two lap records on his fully-faired XR, finishing joint top rider with British Triumph ace Ray Pickrell, and proving once and for all that Americans could ride road-race bikes with the best.

Harley recently produced a very different competition machine in the VR1000, a road-racer whose fuel-injected, watercooled, DOHC eight-valve, 60-degree V-twin engine heralded

a new era for the American firm. With its modern twin-beam aluminium frame, the VR had little apart from its V-twin layout and its colour scheme in common with previous Harleys. The VR was first raced at Daytona in 1994, ridden by Miguel Duhamel, and remained down on power compared to rival Superbikes a year later. But Harley showed no signs of giving up the fight.

HENDERSON

■ BELOW *By 1920s' standards, Henderson's in-line four-cylinder engine was supremely smooth and powerful.*

■ BOTTOM *The KJ model, known as the "Streamline", was a fast, refined and inevitably expensive machine.*

■ HENDERSON KJ

Arguably the finest and most sophisticated machines in the years up to 1930, American-built Hendersons featured four-cylinder engines mounted in-line with the bike. The firm began production in 1911, using the engine layout and long wheelbase format that would become its trademark. Six years later, founder Bill Henderson sold the firm to Schwinn, makers of bicycles and Excelsior motorbikes, and left to found Ace. The Henderson firm continued development, and its 1301cc K model of 1920 produced 28bhp to give an impressive top speed of 80mph (128kph). Among its several advanced features were electric lighting and a fully-enclosed chain.

HENDERSON KJ (1929)

Engine	Aircooled 8-valve inlet-over-exhaust in-line four
Capacity	1301cc
Power	40bhp
Weight	225kg (495lb) approx.
Top speed	100mph (160kph)

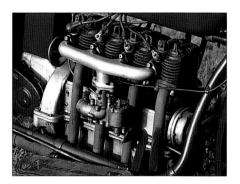

In 1929, Henderson reached new heights of luxury with the Model KJ, known as the "Streamline", which featured improved cooling to a stronger, 40bhp engine of the familiar in-line four-cylinder layout. The Streamline was fast – capable of a genuine 100mph (160kph) – and typically advanced, with leading-link forks and such details as an illuminated speedometer set into the fuel tank. But it failed to sell during America's Depression, and Schwinn halted production in 1931. By then Indian had bought the rights to produce Ace machines, and continued to build its own four into the 1940s.

OTHER MAKES

■ HARRIS

Brothers Steve and Lester Harris set up their chassis firm in Hertford in the 1970s, and made their name with a series of fine-handling café racers, known as the Magnums. These featured Harris-made tubular steel frames, with a range of top-quality cycle parts. Engines were normally Japanese fours, ranging from the Kawasaki Z1000-engined Magnum 1 of the late 1970s to the recent Magnum 4, powered by Suzuki's GSX-R motor.

Throughout the 1980s Harris produced numerous chassis for racing, and developed aluminium beam frames for road and track. In recent years the firm has been heavily involved in 500cc Grands Prix and, along with French company ROC, has worked in conjunction with Yamaha to produce bikes powered by the Japanese factory's V-four engines.

■ HERCULES

After building bicycles for several years, Germany's Hercules produced its first motorbike in 1904. After the Second World War, Hercules concentrated on small-capacity two-strokes with engines from Sachs. The firm rapidly built up a large range of bikes in the 1950s, notably its first twin-cylinder model, the 318. This was billed as a luxury tourer, and had a 247cc engine that produced 12 bhp. Sachs took control of the firm in 1969. The Hercules name survived, notably with the W2000 of the mid-1970s – the world's first commercially built Wankel rotary-engined motorbike. Its 294cc – or 882cc, depending how it was measured – motor produced a claimed 27bhp at 6500rpm and gave a top speed of almost 90mph (145kph). But the rotary, which was marketed as a DKW in Britain, did not sell well, and recent production has been limited to two-stroke motorcycles of below 100cc.

■ RIGHT *The Hercules/DKW W2000 rotary had lively performance but was not a sales success.*

■ FAR RIGHT *Post-war Hercules production concentrated on two-strokes such as this enduro machine.*

■ ABOVE *The Harris Magnum 4 held a four-cylinder Suzuki GSX-R engine in a frame of traditional steel tubes.*

■ LEFT *Steve Harris and brother Lester based their 500cc Grand Prix chassis on Wayne Rainey's factory Yamaha.*

HESKETH

■ HESKETH V1000

When it was launched in 1981, the Hesketh V1000 was billed by its creator as being the finest machine in the world, a two-wheeled Aston Martin which would prove that the British could still build motorcycles. Lord Alexander Hesketh had money, he had run a high-profile Formula One car-racing team, and on paper his handsome V1000 was very promising. Its aircooled, 992cc, 90-degree V-twin engine, designed by four-stroke specialist Weslake, used twin cams and four valves per cylinder to produce an impressive 86bhp. The Hesketh's frame was a neat structure of nickel-plated steel tubing, and it held top quality motorcycle parts including Marzocchi suspension and Brembo disc brakes from Italy.

■ LEFT *When cruising on an open road, the Hesketh felt impressively fast, smooth and relaxed.*

■ BELOW *The V1000's neat bodywork, nickel-plated frame and V-twin engine made an attractive combination.*

■ RIGHT *Numerous problems with its engine and gearbox were the main reason for the V1000's failure.*

■ BELOW *The fully-faired Vampire tourer was as unsuccessful as the V1000.*

HESKETH V1000 (1982)

Engine	Aircooled 8-valve DOHC 90-degree V-twin
Capacity	992cc (95 x 70mm)
Power	86bhp @ 6500rpm
Weight	230kg (506lb) dry
Top speed	120mph (193kph)

Despite an excessive weight of 230kg (506lb), the bike handled and braked very well. It was also reasonably fast and smooth, too, with a top speed of 120mph (192kph) and a pleasantly relaxed cruising feel at 90mph (145kph). But the Hesketh was plagued by problems from the start. In particular, the V-twin engine was noisy, unreliable, leaked oil and suffered from a horribly imprecise and noisy transmission. Production was delayed, faults were slow to be corrected, losses mounted, and Hesketh Motorcycles went bust in May 1982. The following year Lord Hesketh set up a new firm to build a fully-faired Vampire tourer, but most of the faults remained and few were produced.

OTHER MAKES

■ HILDERBRAND & WOLFMÜLLER

The world's first motorcycle to achieve series production was the 1488cc four-stroke built by brothers Heinrich and Wilhelm Hilderbrand, and Alois Wolfmüller. Starting in 1894, the Munich-based partnership produced about 1000 examples of the watercooled parallel twin, which developed 2.5bhp and had a top speed of 25mph (40kph). Normal braking was by a steel spoon that pressed on the front tyre, supplemented if necessary by a large rear bar that could be released to dig into the road. Motorcycling's rapid development at that time meant the twin soon became outdated, and production ended in 1897.

■ HOLDEN

Colonel Sir Henry Capel Holden was one of the great characters of motorcycling's pioneering years. He designed the world's first four-cylinder motorbike, a 1054cc watercooled, flat-four that was built in Coventry between 1899 and 1902. The four-stroke engine produced 3bhp, giving the bicycle-style Holden a top speed of about 25mph (40kph). Colonel Holden went on to design Brooklands, the world's first purpose-built race circuit, in 1906.

■ ABOVE *Hilderbrand & Wolfmüller's 1488cc twin, the world's first production bike, revved to just 240rpm.*

■ ABOVE *As well as designing the world's first four, Holden produced this stem-powered bike in 1898.*

■ BELOW LEFT *For a 305cc parallel twin, the CB77's smoothness and 95mph (152kph) top speed were impressive.*

■ BOTTOM *Honda's CB77 and the similar 247cc CB72 were fast, well-made and reliable machines.*

HONDA

■ HONDA CB77

The world's largest motorcycle manufacturer was founded in October 1946, when Soichiro Honda set up the Honda Technical Research Institute in a small wooden shed in Hamamatsu. Aiming to provide cheap transport for a population hit by defeat in the Second World War, Honda first bolted army-surplus engines to bicycles. A year later he built his own 50cc two-stroke engine, and in 1949 Honda and his 20 employees produced their first complete bike: the 98cc two-stroke Model D, or "Dream". Sales were good, progress was rapid and by 1953 Honda had developed the more sophisticated Model J Benly, whose

90cc four-stroke single-cylinder engine design owed much to Germany's NSU.

The first Hondas to make an impact in export markets were the 250cc CB72 and 305cc CB77 of the early 1960s. Sportier versions of the four-stroke

HONDA CB77 (1963)

Engine	Aircooled 4-valve SOHC parallel twin
Capacity	305cc (60 x 54mm)
Power	28.5bhp @ 9000rpm
Weight	159kg (350lb) dry
Top speed	95mph (152kph)

■ LEFT *Soichiro Honda built and raced cars before starting his bike firm in 1946.*

■ BELOW LEFT *Honda's first complete bike was the 98cc Model D of 1949.*

■ BELOW *Clever advertising made the C100 a success.*

■ BELOW *Much of Honda's success in the 1960s was due to simple, reliable roadsters like this 125cc Benly.*

■ BOTTOM *Although it was neither fast nor successful, the CB450 heralded Honda's big-bike challenge.*

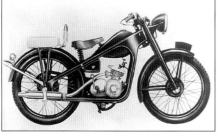

parallel twin C72 and C77 models, the Hondas differed from British twins by using a 180-degree crankshaft, with the pistons rising and falling alternately. Honda's conventional pressed-steel frame, as used on the popular 125cc CB92, was replaced by a tubular steel structure, holding telescopic forks, twin shocks and powerful front and rear drum brakes. With a top speed of 95mph (152kph) and good handling, the CB77– known as the Super Hawk in the States – was a match for many larger British bikes. It was also reliable and oil-tight, and did much for Honda's growing reputation – as did Mike Hailwood's 250cc world championship win in 1961.

Of all Honda's bikes over the years, the most important was arguably the humble C100 Super Cub that was launched in 1958. Combining scooter-style full enclosure with large wheels and an engine placed in the conventional motorbike position instead of under the seat, the Super Cub offered convenience, economy, reliability, cleanliness and even a certain style. Boosted by the famous advertising line,

"You meet the nicest people on a Honda", and by the firm's decision to sell it in American sports and leisure goods shops as well as bike dealerships, the C100 soon became the best-selling motorcycle of all time.

The bike that proved Honda was becoming a major force in motorcycling was the CB450 of 1965. Until the CB's arrival, the Japanese firm had been content to build small-capacity bikes. But with its DOHC, parallel twin engine

displacing 445cc and producing 43bhp, the bike, publicized as the "Black Bomber" or "Black Hawk", was a clear challenge to the long-dominant British twins. In fact, the CB450 turned out to be smooth, comfortable and softly tuned, with a top speed of around 100mph (160kph). Despite respectable handling it couldn't keep up with the British opposition, and was not a great success, but the CB450 signalled the start of Honda's attack on the big bike market.

HONDA

■ HONDA CB750

Modern day motorcycling arrived with Honda's CB750, which offered a new level of performance and sophistication when it was released in 1969. The CB750 was the first mass-produced four-cylinder bike, a fact emphasized by its impressive array of chromed tailpipes, and it incorporated an electric starter, disc front brake and five-speed gearbox, all at a competitive price. The CB750 dominated the early 1970s, became known as the first superbike and had a great influence on machines that followed.

The CB750's major attraction was its 736cc, four-cylinder engine, which was

■ LEFT *The CB750's chassis was less impressive than its engine, but the Honda handled reasonably well.*

■ OPPOSITE *With its four-cylinder engine and front disc brake, the CB750 was in a class of its own in 1969.*

■ BELOW *As well as being powerful, the 736cc four was smooth, reliable, oil-tight and came fitted with an electric starter.*

■ BELOW *Ten years after the first four,*
the 16-valve CB750K was unreliable and
handled very poorly.

■ BOTTOM *Handsome, agile and capable*
of 100mph (160kph), the CB400 was
dubbed the "poor boy's superbike".

■ MIDDLE *Dick Mann's 1970 Daytona-*
winning CB750 is seen here ridden by
racer/journalist Alan Cathcart.

HONDA CB750 (1969)

Engine	Aircooled 8-valve SOHC transverse four
Capacity	736cc (61 x 63mm)
Power	67bhp @ 8000rpm
Weight	218kg (480lb) dry
Top speed	125mph (201kph)

smooth, reliable and produced an impressive 67bhp. Although the four-pot motor was an SOHC, two-valves-per-cylinder design, its development could be traced to Honda's racing exploits with high-revving twin-camshaft fours in the 1960s. The CB750 was a big and rather heavy bike with high handlebars, intended as an all-rounder. But it still whistled to a top speed of about 125mph (201kph), handled reasonably well and sold in huge numbers worldwide.

In the 1970s, Honda did relatively little to uprate the CB750, which meant that it lost ground to newer rivals including Kawasaki's 900cc Z1, which arrived in 1973. The Honda actually lost some performance, as its engine was detuned to reduce emissions. When it was given a facelift to produce the CB750F in 1976, the new bike's flat handlebars, racer styling, vivid yellow paintwork and four-into-one exhaust system were let down by a top speed of below 120mph (193kph). The DOHC, 16-valve CB750K of 1979 had an unreliable engine and poor handling, all of which seemed a far cry from the

brilliance of the original CB750.

Although the CB750's engine formed the basis for many specials and racebikes throughout the 1970s, the Honda made less of an impact on the track than in the showrooms. One racing highlight was veteran American star Dick Mann's victory at Daytona in 1970, which did much to boost the four's image. Some of the most successful straight-four racers were the RCB endurance bikes of the mid-1970s, which dominated long distance events in the hands of riders such as French duo Christian Léon and Jean-Claude Chemarin.

The CB750's success inspired Honda to produce several smaller fours in the 1970s, starting with the CB500 that arrived in 1971, and which was in some respects an even better bike. Its 498cc, 50bhp engine gave a top speed of just over 100mph (160kph), and the CB500's reduced size and weight gave improved handling and manoeuvrability. Honda produced another winner in 1975

with the CB400. Designed mainly for the European market with flat handlebars, sporty styling and a neat four-into-one exhaust system, the CB400 was much loved for its blend of lively performance and taut handling.

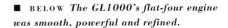

■ BELOW *The GL1000's flat-four engine was smooth, powerful and refined.*

■ BELOW MIDDLE *The Gold Wing name means flying with a first-class ticket.*

■ BOTTOM *Even the original, unfaired GL1000 was a big, fat and heavy bike.*

HONDA

■ HONDA GL1000 GOLD WING

Few bikes provoke such extreme reaction as Honda's Gold Wing. Much more than simply a motorcycle, the large and luxurious Wing has inspired, over two decades of production, a cult following that no other single model can match. Throughout most of that time it has offered unmatched levels of two-wheeled comfort and civility. Yet to many motorcyclists the Wing – always most popular in America, and built in Ohio since 1980 – is merely overweight, overpriced and overrated.

The original, unfaired GL1000 Gold Wing was the world's biggest and heaviest bike when it was introduced in 1975. Most notable for its unique, watercooled flat-four engine, the GL also

HONDA GL1000 GOLD WING (1975)

Engine	Watercooled 8-valve SOHC transverse flat-four
Capacity	999cc (72 x 61.4mm)
Power	80bhp @ 7000rpm
Weight	260kg (571lb) dry
Top speed	122mph (196kph)

featured shaft drive, twin front disc brakes and an under-seat fuel tank. The Wing produced 80bhp, had a top speed of 120mph (193kph), and accelerated hard despite 260kg (571lb) of weight. Its smoothness and comfort rapidly won a large following, especially among middle-aged Americans.

■ LEFT *Its handling was inevitably ponderous, but the GL1000 was unbeatable for relaxed long-distance cruising.*

■ BELOW *Gold Wing riders have traditionally been older and more presentable than the average motorcyclist.*

Many riders fitted accessories to their Gold Wings, prompting Honda to introduce a fully-dressed model in 1980. Called the Interstate in America and the De Luxe in Europe, it combined an enlarged 1100cc engine with a fairing, hard luggage and crash-bars. The bike was a hit, as was the Aspencade – named after a big American rally – that was launched two years later with a sound system, passenger backrest and on-board compressor for the air suspension. Two-wheeled luxury touring

had finally come of age.

For many owners the Gold Wing provides an entry to club runs, rallies and other social events. The two main American Wing owners' clubs each have branches all over the States. Thousands of riders gather together at the annual Wing Ding, for entertainment, custom contests, technical seminars and accessory stands. Similar meetings are called Trefferns in Europe, where there are Gold Wing owners' groups in 15 different countries.

The size and sophistication of the Gold Wing reached new levels in 1988 with the introduction of the GL1500, powered by an all-new flat-six engine. Fully-enclosed, complete with big fairing, built-in luggage, cruise control and an electronic reverse gear to help when parking, the GL1500 was the heaviest and most complex Gold Wing yet. More to the point, it was also the fastest, smoothest and most responsive. For such a huge bike, it also handled and braked remarkably well.

■ ABOVE *Back in 1984, the Aspencade's lavish control console looked like something out of an aeroplane.*

■ RIGHT *For comfortable two-wheeled travel in your old age, nothing could beat the six-cylinder GL1500.*

HONDA

■ HONDA CBX1000

The stunning six-cylinder CBX1000 was released in 1978 to demonstrate Honda's ability to build powerful, race-developed motorbikes. At its heart was an aircooled, 1047cc motor containing twin camshafts and 24 valves. A descendant of Honda's multi-cylinder racers of the 1960s, the engine produced 105bhp to send the CBX accelerating smoothly to a top speed of 135mph (217kph), with a spine-tingling note from its exhaust. The huge powerplant, with six shiny exhaust downpipes jutting from its bank of angled-forward cylinders, was left uncovered by frame tubes for maximum visual effect.

Designed as an out-and-out sports-bike by former Grand Prix engineer Shoichiro Irimajiri, the CBX featured sleek, restrained styling and used its engine as a stressed member of the steel frame. Firm suspension helped give

■ ABOVE *The CBX1000's steel frame was designed to leave the huge six-cylinder engine on show.*

■ BELOW *Despite its high bars, the CBX was a sportsbike by 1978 standards, complete with lean, aggressive styling.*

good handling despite the bike's considerable weight, and no rival superbike could match the Honda's blend of speed, smoothness and six-cylinder soul. Unfortunately that was not enough to make the CBX successful, particularly in the important American market. In 1981 the bike was detuned slightly and fitted with a fairing and single-shock, air-assisted suspension. The CBX-B was a competent sports-tourer, and sold well. But it had none of the raw appeal of the original six.

Arguably Honda's most singleminded roadster of the early 1980s was the CB1100R, an exotic 1062cc straight-four produced in small numbers mainly

■ BELOW *In Ron Haslam's hands, the superb CB1100R made an almost invincible production racer.*

■ BOTTOM *The CX500 Turbo was a magnificent technical achievement, but not an outstanding motorcycle.*

■ BELOW *For such a big, heavy motorcycle, the firmly suspended CBX1000 handled exceptionally well.*

HONDA CBX1000 (1978)

Engine	Aircooled 24-valve DOHC transverse six
Capacity	1047cc (64.5 x 53.4mm)
Power	105bhp @ 9000rpm
Weight	263kg (580lb) dry
Top speed	135mph (217kph)

to win prestigious long-distance production races such as the Castrol Six-Hour in Australia. A development of the CB900, the 1100R combined a tuned, 115bhp engine – the most powerful four-cylinder unit in motorcycling – with an uprated chassis and a racy fairing. Not only was the CB1100R almost unbeatable on the track, but it also made a superb road-going Superbike too.

Among Honda's many innovative bikes of the 1980s was the CX500 Turbo, which was launched in 1981. Less of a practical motorcycle than a corporate statement of engineering expertise, the Turbo used the world's smallest turbocharger to boost the output of the CX500 V-twin – one of the least suitable engine layouts for forced induction – from 50 to 82bhp. The CX chassis was comprehensively redesigned

and given a large fairing. Although heavy, the result was a fast, stable and comfortable sports tourer. But the CX Turbo's performance did not justify its complexity and high price and few riders were tempted to buy one. After first enlarging the engine to produce the CX650 Turbo – and seeing the other three Japanese firms follow with turbo-bikes of their own – Honda abandoned the turbocharging experiment.

HONDA

■ HONDA VFR750F

In the early 1980s Honda produced a series of roadsters powered by four-stroke V-four engines, and the water-cooled, 90-degree layout – which is well-suited to bike use due to its narrow width, smoothness and low centre of gravity – looked set to challenge the transverse four's domination. The VF750F of 1983, in particular, was a fast and fine-handling machine. A year later, Honda's range included five different VF models, from 400 to

HONDA VFR750F (1994)

Engine	Watercooled 16-valve DOHC 90-degree V4
Capacity	748cc (70 x 48.6mm)
Power	100bhp @ 9500rpm
Weight	209kg (460lb) dry
Top speed	150mph (240kph)

1000cc. But the VF750 developed mechanical problems that proved hugely expensive and embarrassing to Honda, and the V-four revolution faded.

In the circumstances the VF's successor, the VFR750F, became one of

the most important bikes Honda has ever produced when it was launched in 1986. Happily for Honda, it was also one of the best. Its V-four motor produced an improved 105bhp, was smooth and flexible and supremely

■ BELOW *The 1994-model VFR, like its predecessors, was arguably the best all-round motorcycle money could buy.*

■ OPPOSITE *The VFR750 has always handled well, despite being less sporty than most of its 750cc rivals.*

■ BELOW *For both performance and race-replica style, the magnificent RC30 was in a class of its own in 1988.*

■ BELOW *Handsome, swift and agile, the VF750 was a fine bike in 1983 – until its engine self-destructed.*

■ BOTTOM *The exotic NR750 had oval pistons and great looks, but it was far too heavy and expensive.*

reliable. The VFR's chassis, based around an all-new aluminium frame, gave good handling. And the Honda's efficient bodywork and high-quality finish contributed to a uniquely well-balanced bike.

The VFR was gradually refined over the next decade, becoming sportier without losing the sophistication and all-round ability that made it unique. Its biggest change came in 1990 with the VFR750FL model, which featured sleeker styling, a stronger, race-derived twin-spar frame and a single-sided swing-arm. Four years later came another revision, with new bodywork and numerous detail changes, but the essential character and appeal of the VFR remained intact.

Honda redefined the limits of sportsbike design with the release of the VFR750R − better known by its code-name RC30 − in 1988. Essentially a road-going copy of the factory RVF racebike that had dominated Formula One and endurance competition in the mid-1980s, the hand-built RC30 was powered by a tuned, 112bhp version of the standard VFR750 engine. The RC30's twin-headlamp fairing, compact layout, light weight and huge twin-beam aluminium frame − rumoured to have been cast in the same dies as the RVF's − made for a super-fast, fine-handling

bike that was virtually unbeatable on both road and track.

The most exotic V-four of all was the oval-pistoned NR750, descendant of the NR500 with which Honda had taken on the two-strokes in 1979, when returning to Grand Prix racing. In 1992, over ten years after abandoning that attempt,

came the gorgeously styled and hugely expensive NR roadster, whose 32-valve motor produced a class-leading 125bhp at 14,000rpm. Its chassis was superb, too, but despite much use of lightweight materials the NR weighed an excessive 222kg (489lb) and was no faster than 750s costing a fraction of the price.

HONDA

■ HONDA CBR600F

The world's most popular bike of recent years has been Honda's CBR600F, which has sold in huge numbers due largely to its ability to provide high performance at a reasonable price. Never intended as a state-of-the-art Superbike, the Honda has nevertheless maintained an excellent balance between power, handling and

HONDA CBR600F (1995)

Engine	Watercooled 16-valve DOHC transverse four
Capacity	599cc (65 x 45.2mm)
Power	100bhp @ 12,000rpm
Weight	185kg (407lb) dry
Top speed	155mph (248kph)

practicality. The CBR's success – over 100,000 were produced in the eight years following its introduction in 1987 – has vindicated Honda's decision to move away from the V-four engine layout, back to the transverse four-cylinder format popularized by the CB750.

The original CBR600F, launched alongside a bigger CBR1000F model with similar fully-enclosed bodywork, was built to compete directly with

Kawasaki's GPZ600 four. Neither Honda model contained much innovative engineering. But the performance of the 600F, in particular – a top speed of 135mph (217kph) from its smooth, 85bhp engine, allied to excellent handling, reasonable comfort and impressive reliability – rapidly

■ BELOW *The 1995-model CBR600F maintained the traditional balance between high performance and reasonable price.*

■ OPPOSITE *Ever since its launch in 1987, the fine-handling CBR600 has been a bestseller all over the world.*

■ BOTTOM *The first CBR900RR's stunning combination of power and light weight made it hugely popular.*

■ RIGHT *Full bodywork has kept both engine and frame hidden since the CBR600F was introduced in 1987.*

■ ABOVE *Honda's CBR1000F, seen here in original 1987 form, has evolved into a fine sports tourer.*

■ BELOW *Few rival Superbikes even approach the FireBlade's speed, either in corners or a straight line.*

established the Honda as the leader in motorcycling's most popular class.

In contrast to the way in which the CB750 was allowed to become decreasingly competitive throughout the 1970s, the CBR600F has repeatedly been refined to keep it at, or near, the head of the pack. An important revision came in 1991, with the introduction of a new 100bhp engine and bodywork restyled to good effect. In 1995 a revised induction system and numerous chassis modifications combined to give improved mid-range performance, top speed of over 150mph (240kph) and even sharper handling.

Like its 600cc sibling, the four-cylinder CBR1000F was designed to provide high performance at an acceptable price – and over the years it has proven to be a very capable sports tourer. The motorcycle's watercooled, 998cc engine has consistently produced over 130bhp with impressive mid-range torque, and its steel-framed chassis, although quite heavy, has given solid handling allied to long-distance comfort. Honda's CBR900RR heralded a new

level of Superbike performance when it was launched in 1992. The CBR, known as the "FireBlade" in most markets, relied on a conventional format of 893cc, 16-valve, straight-four engine and twin-beam aluminium frame. It gained its edge by housing a 123bhp motor – good for a top speed of 165mph (265kph) –

in a motorcycle which, at just 185kg (407lb), weighed less than most 600cc middleweights. The smooth, high-revving motor, racy steering geometry and taut suspension gave a blend of straight-line and cornering speed that no mass-produced machine could match and the FireBlade was another success.

HONDA

■ BELOW *This immaculate RC166, owned by enthusiasts Team Obsolete, has been raced in classic events by Jim Redman.*

■ HONDA RC166 SIX

Soichiro Honda had raced cars with some success before turning to motorcycle production, and knew competition could bring both prestige and technical knowledge. Honda entered some Japanese meetings in the mid-1950s, and in 1959 made a first visit to the Isle of Man TT. The early 125cc racebikes were based on German NSU twins but proved uncompetitive against the dominant MV Agustas, but Honda learned fast. In 1961, aided by MV's retirement from the smaller classes, Honda's Tom Phillis and Mike Hailwood won the 125 and 250cc world championships.

In the next season Honda was even more successful. Swiss star Luigi Taveri won the first of his three 125cc titles, and Jim Redman of Rhodesia took both 250 and 350cc championships. Redman

HONDA RC166 (1967)	
Engine	Aircooled 24-valve DOHC transverse six
Capacity	247cc (39 x 34.5mm)
Power	60bhp @ 18,000rpm
Weight	120kg (264lb) dry
Top speed	153mph (245kph)

went on to win a total of six titles on Honda's fours. But it was the six-cylinder machine, raced to 250 and 350cc championships by Mike Hailwood in both 1966 and 1967 that was Honda's finest four-stroke racebike.

The six was designed to resist Yamaha's increasingly strong two-stroke challenge by allowing very high revs. In 250cc form its compact engine, containing 24 tiny valves, emitted an unforgettable exhaust howl and produced 60bhp at a heady 18,000rpm. The six was debuted prematurely by Redman in late 1964, and improved for both reliability and handling during the following season. In 1966 Hailwood won ten out of 12 Grands Prix on the 250cc RC166, and also took the 350 title on a bored-out 297cc version. Hailwood retained both championships on the six before Honda quit Grand Prix racing in 1968.

Despite success in the smaller classes, Honda could not win the 500cc championship in the 1960s. Mike Hailwood came agonizingly close on a four-cylinder 500 whose handling and reliability did not match its power. In 1966 a breakdown in the final round at Monza cost Hailwood the title, which Giacomo Agostini won for MV Agusta by six points. In the next season's

■ LEFT *Even
Freddie Spencer
could not make the
NR500 competitive
against the 500cc
Grand Prix two-
strokes.*

■ BELOW *Swiss star Luigi Taveri, here in
action on a 250, won three 125cc titles for
Honda in the 1960s.*

■ ABOVE *Mike Hailwood, riding this
250cc six, won the Junior TT on his way to
the world title in 1967.*

■ BELOW *The oval-pistoned, monocoque-
framed NR500 proved uncompetitive when
it was first raced in 1979.*

penultimate race, Hailwood broke the
lap record and led by half a lap –
before his Honda stuck in top gear. Mike
won the final race but Ago took the title
– not on points or even race wins, which
were equal, but on his greater number of
second places.

When Honda returned to Grands Prix
to take on the two-strokes in 1979,
company policy dictated using a four-
stroke. Thus was born the NR500: a
watercooled V-four whose oval pistons –
in fact shaped like running tracks, with
two plugs, two conrods and eight valves

to each cylinder – were intended to give
the next best thing to a V-eight now that
engines had been limited to four
cylinders. The radical bike also used a
monocoque aluminium frame and 16-
inch wheels. Its engine revved to
20,000rpm, but Honda had attempted
too much and the NR was slow and
unreliable. Simplifying the chassis and
redesigning the engine brought
improvements by 1981, but Honda
abandoned the NR that year without
having come close to a Grand Prix win
let alone the championship.

■ ABOVE *Honda's four Japanese riders all
managed respectable placings at the firm's
first Isle of Man TT in 1959.*

HONDA

■ LEFT *Freddie Spencer rode Honda's NS500 triple to the title in 1983.*

■ BELOW *Spencer used Honda's works NSR250 V-twin to complete a championship double in 1985.*

■ HONDA NSR500

After giving up with the four-stroke NR500, Honda finally won a first 500cc world championship with a two-stroke that was almost as unconventional. Freddie Spencer beat the four-cylinder Suzukis and Yamahas in 1983 with the NS500 – a reed-valve triple whose 125bhp output was 10bhp down on the opposition's, but which had an advantage in manoeuvrability. Fast Freddie's second championship, though, was won in 1985 on the bike that would be Honda's weapon for the next decade: the NSR500 V-four.

Since then, the NSR has generally been the most powerful of the factory 500s, partly due to its unique single-crankshaft design which reduces friction but increases width. After unsuccessful experiments with the fuel tank under the engine in 1984, the NSR has used a conventional chassis layout, with an aluminium twin-beam frame. In Honda tradition, the V-four's handling has often failed to match its horsepower – notably in 1989, when Eddie Lawson tamed a wayward NSR to win the title.

HONDA NSR500 (1994)

Engine	Watercooled 112-degree V-four crankcase reed-valve two-stroke
Capacity	499cc (54 x 54.5mm)
Power	187bhp @ 12,000rpm
Weight	130kg (286lb) dry
Top speed	197mph (315kph)

■ OPPOSITE BOTTOM *The NSR500's basic layout has changed little since 1986.*

■ RIGHT *By 1994, Doohan's NSR had the handling to match its traditional horsepower advantage.*

■ BELOW *Eddie Lawson tamed the NSR and won the title in 1989.*

Recent years have seen the gradual evolution of the NSR, the biggest change coming in 1992 with the introduction of the "big bang" engine. Timing its four cylinders to fire in quick succession made the awesome 185bhp NSR easier to ride, a trick quickly copied by rival teams. Japanese ace Shinichi Itoh was the first Grand Prix rider to be timed at 200mph (320kph), on an NSR500 at Germany's Hockenheim in 1993. In the following season Australian Mick Doohan overcame the effects of a serious leg injury, sustained two years earlier, to dominate the championship on the NSR.

Honda found more success after effectively cutting the 500cc V-four motor in half to produce the NSR250 V-twin. Championship wins included Sito Pons' double in 1988 and 1989, and Luca Cadalora's in 1991 and 1992. Perhaps the finest achievement was by Freddie Spencer, who won both 500 and 250cc titles on NSRs in 1985.

OTHER MAKES

■ HOREX
A leading German make for many years, Horex was founded in 1923 and built many sophisticated road and race bikes in the following years. The firm's most successful model was the Regina, a 350cc OHV single, produced from the late 1940s. The 400cc Imperator, a stylish and technically advanced SOHC parallel twin introduced in 1951, featured telescopic or leading-link forks, twin-shock rear suspension and an enclosed drive chain.

Horex hit problems in the mid-1950s, partly due to the disastrous 250cc Rebell scooter, and the factory closed in 1958. In the 1970s, Friedel Münch and fellow enthusiast Fritz Roth attempted to revive the name with a 1400cc turbocharged

■ FAR LEFT *Former racer Sammy Miller on Husqvarna's 1930's V-twin in a TT classic parade.*

four, based on Münch's Mammut, and a series of small-capacity two-strokes. More recently the Horex name was used on a Honda 650cc single-cylinder engined sportster called the Osca, which was built and sold in Japan.

■ HRD
Howard Raymond Davies was a racer and former First World War air ace who in 1924 set up a firm to build bikes under his own name. The following year Davies won the Senior TT on an HRD, and Freddie Dixon scored a Junior win two years later. But roadster sales were disappointing, and the firm went into liquidation shortly afterwards. The HRD name was later bought by Philip Vincent, to add credibility to his own machines.

■ HUSQVARNA
Best known in recent years for motocross and enduro bikes, Swedish firm Husqvarna was an armaments firm that diversified into motorcycle production in 1903. In the 1930s the firm built innovative 350 and 500cc V-twins that were raced successfully by riders including Stanley Woods. Husqvarna continued to build successful off-road competition machines after roadster production was ended in the early 1960s. In 1986 the firm became part of the Cagiva Group, and Husqvarna production was moved to Italy.

■ ABOVE *French rider Vuillemin corners his twin-cylinder Horex in a classic event.*

■ ABOVE *Husqvarna rider Jan Carlsson in the 1983 International Six Days Enduro.*

INDIAN

INDIAN POWERPLUS

Indian was founded in 1901 by George Hendee and Oscar Hedstrom, two former bicycle racers, who teamed up to produce a 1.75bhp single in Hendee's home town of Springfield. The bike was successful, and sales increased dramatically during the next decade. In 1904, the so-called diamond framed Indian single, whose engine was built by the Aurora firm in Illinois, was made available in the deep red colour that would become Indian's trademark. By now production was up to over 500 bikes annually, and would rise to a best-ever 32,000 in 1913.

In 1907, Indian built its first V-twin, and in following years made a strong showing in racing and record-breaking. One of the firm's most famous riders was Erwin "Cannonball" Baker, who set many long-distance records. In 1914, he rode an Indian across America, from San Diego to New York, in a record 11 days,

■ ABOVE *The power and refinement of Indian's new side-valve engine earned it the name Powerplus.*

INDIAN POWERPLUS (1918)	
Engine	Aircooled 4-valve 42-degree V-twin
Capacity	998cc (79.4 x 100.8mm)
Power	18bhp
Weight	186kg (410lb) wet
Top speed	60mph (96kph)

12 hours and ten minutes. Baker's mount in subsequent years was the Powerplus, a side-valve V-twin that was introduced in 1916. Its 61ci (1000cc), 42-degree V-twin engine was more powerful and quieter than previous designs, giving a top speed of 60mph (96kph). The Powerplus was highly successful, both as a roadster and as the basis for racing bikes. It remained in production with few changes until 1924.

■ BELOW *The 1918-model Powerplus had only minor differences from the machine introduced two years earlier.*

■ LEFT *In 1904 Indian's single offered a 30mph (48kph) top speed, excellent build quality and optional red finish.*

■ BELOW *This 1913-model Indian V-twin has the earlier F-head (or inlet-over-exhaust) valve layout.*

Competition success played a big part in Indian's rapid growth, and spurred technical innovation. One of the American firm's best early results came in the Isle of Man TT in 1911, when Indian riders Godfrey, Franklin and Moorehouse finished first, second and third. Indian star Jake De Rosier set several speed records both in America and at Brooklands in England, and won an estimated 900 races, on dirt-tracks and boards. He left Indian for Excelsior and died in 1913, aged 33, of injuries sustained in a board-race crash with Charles "Fearless" Balke, who later became Indian's top rider. Work at the Indian factory was stopped while De Rosier's funeral procession passed.

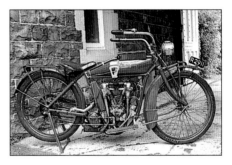

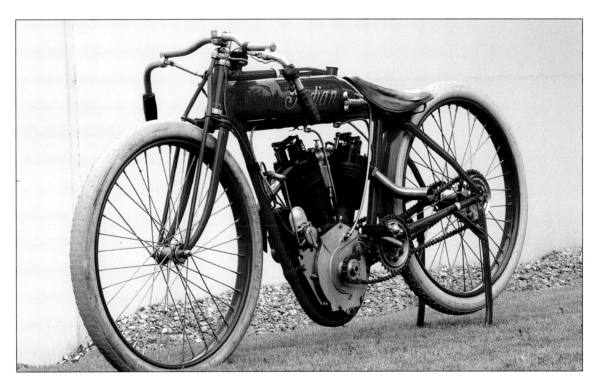

■ RIGHT *Indian's powerful eight-valve racers were very successful on the American tracks in 1916.*

INDIAN

■ INDIAN CHIEF

The Scout and Chief V-twins, introduced
in the early 1920s when Indian could
claim to be the world's largest motorcycle manufacturer, became the Springfield firm's most successful models.
Designed by Charles B Franklin, the
middleweight Scout and larger Chief
shared a 42-degree V-twin engine

INDIAN CHIEF (1947)

Engine	Aircooled 4-valve sidevalve 42-degree V-twin
Capacity	1200cc (82.5 x 113mm)
Power	40bhp @ 4000rpm
Weight	245kg (539lb) dry
Top speed	85mph (136kph)

■ ABOVE *The 1200cc Big Chief was
introduced in 1923, and immediately
outsold Indian's smaller Scout model.*

■ RIGHT *Almost all Indian V-twin engines,
including this 74ci (1200cc) unit, had a
42-degree cylinder angle.*

■ BELOW *This 1947-model Chief, with
headdress mascot on its skirted front
fender, epitomizes the Indian look.*

■ **ABOVE FAR RIGHT** *Scouts were raced successfully for many years, and still compete in classic events.*

■ **RIGHT** *The 500cc (30.5ci) Scout Pony, seen here in 1939 form, was aimed at the entry-level rider.*

■ **BELOW RIGHT** *The Model 741 Military Scout served with distinction in the Second World War.*

layout. Both models gained a reputation for strength and reliability, which led to the old Indian saying: "You can't wear out an Indian Scout, or its brother the Indian Chief. They're built like rocks to take hard knocks; it's the Harleys that cause the grief."

The first 1922 model Chief had a 1000cc (61ci) engine based on that of the Powerplus; a year later the engine was enlarged to 1200cc (73ci). Numerous improvements were made over the years, including adoption of a front brake in 1928. After Indian had been bought by E Paul DuPont in 1930, the new owner's paint industry connections resulted in no fewer than 24 colour options being offered in 1934. Models of that era featured Indian's famous head-dress logo on the gas tank. Indian's huge Springfield factory was known as the Wigwam, and native American imagery was much used in advertising.

In 1940 all models were fitted with the large skirted fenders that became an

Indian trademark, and the Chief gained a new sprung frame that was superior to rival Harley's unsprung rear end. The 1940s Chiefs were handsome and comfortable machines, capable of 85mph (136kph) in standard form and over 100mph (160kph) when tuned, although their increased weight

hampered acceleration. In 1950, the V-twin engine was enlarged to 1300cc (80ci) and telescopic forks were adopted. But Indian's financial problems meant that few bikes were built, and production of the Chief ended in 1953.

The Scout, initially with a 596cc (37ci) engine that was bored-out to 745cc (45ci) in 1927, rivalled the Chief as Indian's most important model. The most famous version was the 101 Scout of 1928, which featured improved handling from a new, lower frame. In 1932, cost-cutting led to the Scout using the heavier Chief frame, which was less successful. Many Scouts were used in the Second World War, but the model was dropped when civilian production restarted in 1946. In 1948, Indian built just 50 units of the Daytona Sports Scout, one of which took Floyd Emde to victory in that year's Daytona 200-mile (322-kilometre) race. Smaller, 500cc (30.5ci) Scouts were also built between 1932 and 1941, known as the Scout Pony, Junior Scout and Thirty-Fifty.

INDIAN

■ INDIAN FOUR

The Indian Four is one of the most famous American motorcycles, though it was by no means one of the most successful. Indian bought the Ace firm, makers of a 1265cc in-line four, in 1927, and the first Indian Four was simply an Ace with smaller wheels and Indian badges. In subsequent years Indian improved the design with a front brake, new forks and a new frame, before introducing the Model 436 Four in 1936. Known as the "upside down" Four because its valvegear was reversed to put intake valves at the side of the engine and exhausts above, the Model 436 was unreliable and short-lived.

Indian returned to the original engine layout and added other improvements in 1938. An early 1940s Four produced 40bhp, was very smooth and had a top speed of 90mph (144kph). But the price was high, rear cylinder overheating remained a problem, and the Four tied up money that Indian might have better spent on developing an overhead-valve V-twin rival to Harley's 61E. Production of the Four eventually ended in 1943.

INDIAN FOUR (1942)

Engine	Aircooled 8-valve sidevalve longitudinal four
Capacity	1265cc (69.9 x 82.5mm)
Power	40bhp @ 5000rpm
Weight	255kg (561lb) dry
Top speed	90mph (144kph)

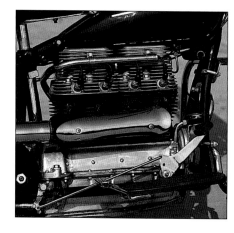

■ OPPOSITE *Factory windshield was a popular accessory for both the Four and Chief in the 1940s.*

■ BELOW LEFT *The in-line four motor was handsome and smooth, but had a tendency to overheat.*

■ BELOW *This well-used Four, built in 1941, has been updated with later forks and foot gearchange.*

Indian's decision to build middleweight vertical twins in the late 1940s also contributed to its demise. The verticals were unreliable and unpopular, and production at Springfield ceased in 1953. Indian continued in business by importing British machines, notably the Royal Enfields which were sold as Indians. The firms split in 1960, after which Indian sold Matchless bikes for a few years before ceasing trading.

The Indian name was also used to sell small Italian-made bikes in the late 1960s and 1970s. More recently, two rival American firms claimed rights to the name and announced plans to build modern V-twins. Those came to nothing, but in 1994 the Indian name was acquired by Australian entrepreneur Maurits Hayim-Langridge. He appointed New Zealander engineer John Britten as a consultant, and announced development of a range of V-twin roadsters to be produced in America by 1998.

OTHER MAKES

■ JAMES

Starting out as a bicycle firm in the last century, Birmingham-based James built four-stroke singles and large-capacity V-twins in the 1930s. In the 1960s, production was based on two-strokes, notably the 250cc Commodore single and its twin-cylinder successor the Superswift. The firm also built a number of trials bikes, and ran a factory team for many years. James became part of AMC in 1963, and ceased production when the group collapsed three years later.

■ ABOVE *The Superswift, introduced in 1962 and powered by a 250cc Villiers two-stroke engine, was one of the last and best James roadsters.*

■ JAWA

Jawa was founded in Czechoslovakia in 1929 and built numerous road and race bikes before the Second World War. Production continued after 1945, in conjunction with CZ, most notably with simple two-stroke roadsters. Jawa also built many highly successful speedway bikes, after taking over the Eso factory in 1962.

■ ABOVE *This 350cc two-stroke from the mid-1960s is a typical Jawa – competent, cheap and strangely styled.*

■ KAHENA

Powered by a 1600cc, flat-four VW car engine producing 50bhp, the Brazilian Kahena was a huge, fully-faired tourer built for the growing South American market of the early 1990s.

KAWASAKI

■ KAWASAKI 500cc H1

The motorcycle division forms a relatively small part of Kawasaki Heavy Industries, a vast firm that produces trains, boats and planes. Kawasaki's involvement with bikes began in the 1950s, when the aircraft division was looking for civilian work, and was stepped up when the industrial giant wanted to increase awareness of its name. In 1960 Kawasaki built its first complete bike, a 125cc two-stroke, and took over Meguro, Japan's oldest motorcycle manufacturer, which had been making copies of British bikes including the BSA A7 parallel twin.

Kawasaki moved into the big bike market in 1966 with the W1, a 650cc

■ LEFT *High bars and sleek styling give this American-market H1-B a deceptively docile look.*

■ OPPOSITE LEFT *The H1's two-stroke triple engine was compact, powerful and very thirsty.*

■ OPPOSITE MIDDLE *The production of triples formed just a tiny part of Kawasaki Heavy Industries' work.*

■ OPPOSITE RIGHT *Kawasaki's first big bikes were 650cc parallel twins such as this W1 SS, produced in 1968.*

■ RIGHT *The fearsome 748cc H2 triple had similar looks to the H1, plus even more power, noise and speed.*

twin, which again owed much to BSA. It sold well in Japan, but flopped against the quicker British bikes on the American market. Kawasaki's response came with lighter, smaller-capacity two-strokes, the 250cc A1 Samurai and similar 350cc A7 Avenger, which were exported more successfully. In 1969 Kawasaki released the 500cc H1, the first of the triples that would earn the firm a well-deserved reputation for outrageous high performance.

With a peak output of 60bhp at 7500rpm from its aircooled, two-stroke engine, and a weight of just 174kg (383lb), the H1 – also known as the Mach III – had an unmatched power-to-weight ratio. It looked good, scorched to

KAWASAKI 500cc H1 (1969)

Engine	Aircooled two-stroke transverse triple
Capacity	499cc (60 x 58.8mm)
Power	60bhp @ 7500rpm
Weight	174kg (383lb)
Top speed	120mph (192km/h)

a top speed of 120mph (192kph), and had handling that made life just a little exciting. The combination of an insubstantial frame, rearwards weight distribution and an abrupt power step at 6000rpm were responsible for introducing the words "wheelie" and "tankslapper" to motorcyclists' vocabularies. Poor fuel economy completed the triple's antisocial image, but owners could live with that.

Kawasaki also built two smaller triples, the 250cc S1 and 350cc S2, and in 1972 enlarged the three-cylinder engine to 748cc to produce the H2, or Mach IV. Its 74bhp motor gave blistering acceleration and a top speed of 125mph (201kph). Handling was slightly better than the H1's, but the H2 was a wild ride and remained so until emissions regulations finally killed off the big two-strokes in the mid-1970s.

KAWASAKI

■ KAWASAKI Z1

Kawasaki's Z1 was released in 1973 and dominated superbiking for much of the decade with its combination of powerful, unburstable motor, handsome looks and competitive price. The Z1's four-cylinder, 903cc engine featured twin camshafts, unlike Honda's SOHC CB750-four, and produced a maximum of 82bhp to give the Kawasaki a top speed of 130mph (208kph). Its straight-line performance outclassed that of the

Honda, whose launch in late 1968 had caused Kawasaki's engineers to delay and revise their four-cylinder project, code-named "New York Steak", which had originally been designed as a 750.

The Z1's chassis did not come close to matching the brilliance of its engine, but the Kawasaki handled reasonably well and was quite comfortable despite high handlebars. Its styling was superb, with a rounded tank, rear ducktail and four shiny silencers. Best of all, the Z1 was far cheaper than rival European

KAWASAKI Z1 (1973)

Engine	Aircooled 8-valve DOHC transverse four
Capacity	903cc (66 x 66mm)
Power	82bhp @ 8500rpm
Weight	230kg (506lb) dry
Top speed	130mph (208kph)

■ ABOVE *The twin-cam Z1 motor was superbly strong and powerful.*

■ BELOW *Strong styling matched the Z1's awesome performance.*

sdfdf
sdfsdfx

■ LEFT *Smaller aircooled Kawasaki fours included the fast and practical Z650, introduced in 1977.*

■ LEFT *Although it was prone to wobbles at high speeds, the Z1 went round slower corners quite well.*

■ BELOW *The Z1-R, with a tuned motor and uprated handling, faced fierce competition in 1978.*

superbikes. It became massively popular, acquired the nickname the "King" and earned Kawasaki a lasting reputation for horsepower and reliability.

Improvements in subsequent years included the addition of a second front disc brake in 1976, when the bike was renamed the Z900. A year later its engine was enlarged to 1015cc to produce the Z1000. In 1978 Kawasaki produced the Z1-R café racer, which featured a tuned, 90bhp engine, strengthened frame and angular styling incorporating a handlebar fairing. It was the best big "Zed" yet but faced renewed opposition from Suzuki's GS1000 and Honda's CBX1000.

The Z1's speed and reliability made it a natural for many forms of racing. In standard form the Kawasaki won Australia's prestigious Castrol Six-Hour race in 1973. In Europe the four-cylinder motor was used to power many endurance racers, notably the factory-backed bikes on which Frenchmen Georges Godier and Alain Genoud won several 24-hour events in the 1970s.

In the late 1970s and early 1980s Kawasaki also built several smaller fours whose layout followed the Z1's pattern. Among the best was the Z650, released in 1977, which provided typically smooth, reliable 110mph (177kph) performance with manoeuvrability and a competitive price. But although Kawasaki had billed the bike as being the 650 that would outperform any 750, they had not reckoned on Suzuki's faster GS750, which was launched at the same time.

■ ABOVE *French ace Jean-Claude Chemarin led Kawasaki's endurance team to success in the early 1980s.*

■ ABOVE *New Zealander Graeme Crosby won races and fans on a high-barred Moriwaki Kawasaki.*

KAWASAKI

■ **LEFT** *Cornering was never going to be the Z1300's strength, but for such a big bike it handled well.*

■ KAWASAKI Z1300

The huge six-cylinder Kawasaki Z1300 was in some ways the ultimate late 1970s Superbike, the inevitable end product of the Japanese manufacturers' race towards bigger, heavier and more complex machines. Its watercooled, 1286cc engine produced a highest-yet 120bhp, and the slab-sided Z1300 weighed over 300kg (661lb) with fuel. Yet, ironically, its large radiator meant the Kawasaki had little of the visual impact of Honda's six-cylinder CBX1000, and the Z1300's performance was less startling than its specification suggested.

Despite all its weight, the Z1300 handled reasonably well, thanks to a

■ **RIGHT** *With an output of 100bhp, Kawasaki's six was motorcycling's most powerful engine in 1979.*

■ **BELOW** *The Z1300's styling and sheer bulk made the six-cylinder engine look almost ordinary.*

KAWASAKI Z1300 (1979)	
Engine	Watercooled 12-valve DOHC transverse six
Capacity	1286cc (62 x 71mm)
Power	120bhp @ 8000rpm
Weight	305kg (670lb) wet
Top speed	135mph (217kph)

strong frame and good suspension, and remained stable all the way to its impressive 135mph (217kph) top speed. But the Kawasaki's exposed, upright riding position limited its high-speed cruising ability, and the six-cylinder motor had a rather busy feel. Despite its unmatched power and bulk the Z1300 offered nothing that several smaller, simpler and cheaper bikes could not provide. The expensive six marked the end of Japan's apparent belief that bigger was better.

One of the outstanding bikes of the 1980s was Kawasaki's GPZ900R, the firm's first watercooled four, which was released in 1984. The GPZ's 908cc,

16-valve engine produced 113bhp at 9500rpm, and was impressively strong in best four-cylinder Kawasaki tradition. It pulled the GPZ smoothly to a top speed of over 150mph (241kph), aided by the excellent aerodynamics of the sharply styled full fairing.

A compact, light chassis provided handling to match, making the "Ninja", as the bike was known in America, hard to beat both on the road and in production racing. Better still, the GPZ matched its speed with genuine long-distance comfort. It immediately became popular and was still being sold almost ten years later having outlasted its supposed successor, the GPZ1000RX.

KAWASAKI

■ KAWASAKI ZZ-R1100

In the ultra-competitive motorcycle world of the 1990s, it was some achievement for Kawasaki to produce a Superbike whose awesome 145bhp powerplant and 175mph (280kph) top speed simply blew away all opposition. Not only did the ZZ-R1100 make just such an impact when it was launched in 1990, but the watercooled, 1052cc

■ OPPOSITE ABOVE *Handling was good, despite the 22-R1100's size and weight.*

■ OPPOSITE BELOW *The 1993-model ZZ-R1100 had a revised chassis, but its engine remained the star attraction.*

■ RIGHT *With a potent 600cc engine and twin-spar alloy frame, the 1995-model ZX-6R was a fast and agile sportster.*

KAWASAKI ZZ-R1100 (1990)

Engine	Watercooled 16-valve DOHC transverse four
Capacity	1052cc (76 x 58mm)
Power	145bhp @ 9500rpm
Weight	228kg (502lb) dry
Top speed	175mph (280kph)

■ ABOVE *Scott Russell won the 1993 World Superbike title and three Daytonas.*

Kawasaki was still the world's fastest production streetbike five years later.

Its straight-line performance came from a 16-valve engine developed from that of the 1988 model ZX-10. Big valves and lightened pistons increased power but the real boost came from the ZZ-R's ram-air system, based on Formula One car-race technology, which ducted cool air from a slot in the fairing nose to a pressurized airbox. The faster the Kawasaki went, the deeper it breathed – with thrilling result.

The ZZ-R was also a smooth and refined motorcycle that handled well thanks to a highly rigid aluminium frame and very good suspension. Heavy at 228kg (502lb), and with a fairly upright riding position, the Kawasaki made a practical and genuinely comfortable sports tourer, and on a straight road, it showed a clean pair of silencers to any other standard motorcycle.

■ ABOVE *High performance and bold styling made the original ZXR750 a big hit.*

Kawasaki's entrant in the 750cc sportsbike class in recent years has been the ZXR750. Conventional in layout – holding a watercooled, 16-valve engine in a twin-beam aluminium frame – the ZXR has consistently provided aggressive looks and 150mph (241kph) performance to match. It has also formed the basis of Kawasaki's World Superbike challenge, which reached a peak with Scott Russell's championship win in 1993.

Having popularized the 600cc class with the GPZ600 in 1985, Kawasaki spent the following years failing to match the sales success of Honda's CBR600F. The ZZ-R600, launched in 1990, provided big bike speed but lacked agility. The 1995 model ZX-6R – featuring ram-air induction and a new aluminium beam frame and sportier geometry – was outstanding, combining speed with superb handling.

KAWASAKI

■ LEFT *Australian star Gregg Hansford was fast and spectacular on the screaming KR750 triple.*

■ BELOW *Removing the KR's fairing reveals its transverse triple engine and twin-cradle steel frame.*

■ KAWASAKI KR750

Kawasaki's first international racing success came in the 125cc class, when Dave Simmonds won the world championship in 1969 on a factory-backed twin. The firm's fearsome two-stroke triple roadsters were naturals for racing, and a competition version of the 500cc H1, the H1R, took New Zealander Ginger Malloy to second

KAWASAKI KR750 (1975)

Engine	Watercooled two-stroke transverse triple
Capacity	747cc (68 x 68mm)
Power	120bhp @ 9500rpm
Weight	140kg (308lb) dry
Top speed	180mph (288kph)

■ BELOW *Mick Grant's KR750, wearing his favourite No. 10 plate, was timed at over 180mph (289kph) at the TT in 1975.*

■ LEFT *Germany's Anton Mang won four world titles on the KR250 and 350 tandem twins in the early 1980s.*

■ LEFT *Even the fast and stylish Kork Ballington could not make the KR500 square-four a Grand Prix winner.*

place in the 500cc world championship in 1970. The later 750cc H2R triples became known as "Green Meanies" after their lime-green colours and dubious handling. American star Gary Nixon and Canadian Yvon Duhamel tamed the triple to take several big wins.

In 1975 Kawasaki replaced the roadster-based H2R with a purpose-built racer, the KR750. This was an all-new triple whose watercooled engine produced a considerably increased 120bhp, with a pronounced power step at 6000rpm that made the bike difficult to ride. Despite early reliability problems Mick Grant and Gregg Hansford were very successful on the KR in 1975, in Britain and Australia respectively. In that season Grant was timed at over 180mph (283kph) as he set a new Isle of Man TT lap record of 109.82mph (176.73kph). The following year privateer Gary Nixon led the F750 world championship on a KR, but controversially finished second after one of the rounds he had won was discounted.

Kawasaki's most successful racebikes were the KR250 and KR350, water-cooled two-stroke tandem twins that dominated Grand Prix racing between

1978 and 1982, winning no fewer than eight world championships and 73 Grands Prix. The KR was introduced in 250cc form in 1975, but initially proved unreliable. Its engine was then re-designed with a 360-degree crankshaft, where pistons rose together, instead of the original 180-degree layout. The new KRs were reliable and very fast, producing a maximum of 75bhp at 11,800rpm in 350cc form. They also handled well thanks to a chassis that included a rigid frame of chrome-moly-bdenum steel tubes, and Kawasaki's Uni-Trak rising-rate rear suspension.

South African Kork Ballington began the KR's domination, winning both 250 and 350cc titles in 1978 and 1979. Germany's Anton Mang added two further titles on each bike, including a double in 1981, and the KR350 retired as undefeated champion when the larger class was dropped after the 1982 season. By then Kawasaki had moved up to 500cc Grand Prix racing with the four-cylinder KR500, which featured an innovative aluminium monocoque chassis. Despite persevering for several seasons, however, even Ballington could not make it competitive.

LAVERDA

■ LAVERDA JOTA 1000

Motorcycles were just a sideline for a large agricultural machinery firm from north-eastern Italy when Francesco Laverda built his first bikes – tiny 75cc four-strokes – in the late 1940s. Small-capacity Laverdas were raced successfully in long-distance events such, as the Milano-Taranto and Giro d'Italia, in the 1950s, but the firm's later concentration on humble, economical bikes coincided with the rise of cheap cars, such as the Fiat 500, and nearly proved disastrous.

Laverda changed tack just in time in the late 1960s, releasing a 650cc four-stroke parallel twin that was quickly enlarged to produce the successful 750GT tourer and 750S sportster. Handsome, rugged and quick, especially the

■ ABOVE *The Jota's greatest asset was its powerful 981cc, three-cylinder engine.*

■ BELOW *Muscular looks and performance to match made the Jota one of the greatest superbikes of the 1970s.*

LAVERDA JOTA 1000 (1976)	
Engine	Aircooled 6-valve DOHC transverse triple
Capacity	981cc (75 x 74mm)
Power	90bhp @ 8000rpm
Weight	236kg (520lb) wet
Top speed	140mph (225kph)

later 750SF models, the twins earned Laverda a growing reputation for performance. Best and fastest of all was the exotic SFC, basically a road-going endurance racer with half-fairing, bright orange paint and tuned engine. Laverda also built an exotic V-six racebike, which was timed at 176mph (283kph) before retiring in its first and only ever

■ ABOVE *Enlarging the mighty three-cylinder powerplant's capacity to 1200cc gave even more mid-range grunt.*

■ ABOVE *The SFC1000 of 1985, the last of the aircooled triples, could not save Laverda from financial disaster.*

■ ABOVE *In 1994, under new management, Laverda began production of the parallel twin 650 sportster.*

■ ABOVE *Laverda's legendary 1000cc V-six racer proved fast but fragile in its only ever appearance in 1978.*

■ LEFT *The exotic, half-faired SFC750 parallel twin of the 1970s was basically an endurance racer built for the road.*

race, the Bol d'Or 24-Hours in 1978.

It was for three-cylinder sportsters, however, that the firm from Breganze became most famous. The first DOHC, 981cc triple, called the 3C, was powerful, good-looking and fairly successful when introduced in 1973. Three years later, at the request of the British Laverda importer, the factory tuned the motor with hot cams, high-compression pistons and free-breathing exhausts to produce the Jota. This was a big, raw 90bhp beast that bellowed to a top speed of 140mph (225kph) and needed a firm hand on the reins. The Jota was aggressive, demanding and expensive. In the mid-1970s it was the fastest thing on two wheels, as numerous production race victories confirmed.

The triple was modified in various ways in following years, without ever matching the success of the original Jota. The 1000cc sportster gained a fairing and a smoother-running, 120-degree crankshaft engine. A 1200cc version was also built, largely for the American market. Tightening emissions legislation prompted the quieter, less aggressive RGS and RGA triples of the 1980s. But although they performed well, prices were high, sales were disappointing and Laverda found itself in financial problems that led to receivership in 1987.

Several new Laverda operations rose only to fall again in the following years until finally, in 1994, production started once again at a new factory in nearby Zane, of the 650 – a model that had been developed several years earlier. This featured a 70bhp parallel twin engine, modern twin-beam aluminium frame and stylish full fairing, and was a fairly quick and agile sportster. Meanwhile Laverda's engineers were planning a new generation watercooled 1000cc triple to take the firm into the 21st century.

OTHER MAKES

■ **LEVIS**
Between 1911 and its demise in 1940, British firm Levis built many two- and four-stroke roadsters. Racing successes included victory in the 1922 Lightweight TT, and later wins in trials and motocross.

■ ABOVE *Levis produced this attractive 500cc four-stroke roadster in 1938.*

MATCHLESS

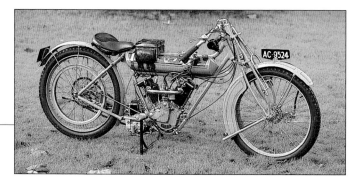

■ MATCHLESS G50

One of the great names of motorcycling's early years, Matchless was founded by the Collier family at Plumstead in south London in 1899. Brothers Charlie and Harry Collier were leading racers, Charlie winning the single-cylinder

MATCHLESS G50 (1961)	
Engine	Aircooled 2-valve SOHC single
Capacity	496cc (90 x 78mm)
Power	51bhp @ 7200rpm
Weight	132kg (290lb) dry
Top speed	135mph (217kph)

■ BELOW LEFT *Good looks and comfort were not enough to make the 400cc Silver Arrow V-twin of 1930 a success.*

■ BOTTOM *The legendary G50 single lived up to its "winged M" badge, winning races throughout the 1960s.*

event at the first ever Isle of Man TT on a Matchless in 1907, and Harry following with a victory two years later. Matchless took over the Wolverhampton-based AJS firm in 1931, and many later models of motorcycles were produced as both AJS and Matchless machines, with very few differences.

In 1930, Matchless released the Silver Arrow, a 400cc V-twin designed by Charlie Collier, but its performance was mediocre and sales poor. Younger brother Bert took over to produce the Silver Hawk, with a more powerful 600cc V-four engine, but despite 80mph (128kph) top speed it could not compete with Ariel's Square Four and was another failure. Matchless had more success with singles, such as the 350cc G3L that was produced in huge numbers for military use in the Second World War. This was one of the first bikes to use telescopic forks, and was later adapted for civilian use in models such as the G3LS of 1959.

The most famous Matchless was the G50 single-cylinder racer, basically a 500cc version of the 350cc AJS 7R. The G50 was first seriously produced in 1959, as a rival to Norton's Manx. Although slightly less powerful, with its 50bhp engine giving a top speed of about 135mph (217kph), the Matchless was lighter and had the edge on twisty circuits. AMC, which Matchless had become part of in 1938, suffered financial problems and went bust in 1966, after which rights to G50 production were bought by Colin Seeley, who continued engine development and built his own chassis to create the Seeley G50. The four-stroke single G50 held its own against the two-strokes until the 1970s, and in recent years has been competitive in classic racing.

■ RIGHT *Colin Seeley bought rights to G50 production and built the Seeley G50, still a force in classic racing.*

OTHER MAKES

■ MAICO

Best known for its highly successful two-stroke motocross and enduro machines, German firm Maico began production in 1933 and built trials and road race bikes, notably the 125cc machines on which Borge Jansson won several Grands Prix in the early 1970s. Roadsters such as the twin-cylinder 350 and 400cc Taifun models were popular in the 1950s. In later years Maico concentrated on dirt bikes, before going bust in 1987.

■ MAGNI

Arturo Magni, team manager of the all-conquering MV Augusta race team, set up in business under his own name after MV's closure in the mid-1970s. Magni

■ ABOVE *In the 1960s, Maico built some rapid small-capacity road-racers.*

produced chassis kits for MV roadsters, and then complete bikes based around Honda's CB900 four. Later Magnis have used Moto Guzzi's V-twin engine, notably the retro-styled Sfida and the sleek, fully-faired Australia sportster.

■ MARUSHO

A leading Japanese manufacturer in the 1950s and early 1960s, Marusho was best known for its Lilac range of 125, 250 and 300cc V-twins. The firm produced a series of flat-twin roadsters before going out of business in the late 1960s.

■ LEFT *Magni's Guzzi-engined Australia sportster was fast and stylish.*

MONDIAL

■ **BELOW** *Mike Hailwood raced a pair of ex-works 250cc Mondials with great success in 1959 and 1960.*

■ MONDIAL 250cc RACER

Small Italian firm FB Mondial produced some fast and beautifully engineered racebikes in the 1950s, its finest moments coming when Tarquinio Provini and Cecil Sandford won the 125 and 250cc world championships in 1957. The company's origins dated back to 1929, when the four Boselli brothers founded FB to sell other firms' bikes. The first Mondials, built at FB's Bologna workshop, were DOHC, single-cylinder 125s. They were immediately successful, winning the world title for three years after its inception in 1949.

■ **BELOW** *Cecil Sandford won the TT and the 250cc world title in 1957 on this twin-cam Mondial single.*

MONDIAL 250cc (1957)	
Engine	Aircooled 2-valve DOHC single
Capacity	249cc (75 x 56.4mm)
Power	29bhp @ 10,800rpm
Weight	125kg (275lb) dry
Top speed	135mph (216kph)

Mondial also produced roadsters, starting with a 125cc four-stroke that was introduced in 1950, but the firm's main interest remained in racing. After

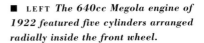

OTHER MAKES

■ MARS

The most memorable of several manufact-urers called Mars was the German firm that produced a 959cc flat-twin roadster, the MA20, which featured an innovative pressed-steel frame in the 1920s. Mars built small-capacity two-strokes until ceasing production in the late 1950s.

■ MEGOLA

One of the strangest motorbikes of all time, the Munich-built Megola was powered by a radial five-cylinder engine situated inside its front wheel. Almost as unusual was the sheet-steel frame, which gave an armchair riding position. The 640cc side-valve motor produced 10bhp, and in sports form the single-speed Megola was timed at 90mph (144kph). Despite its unconventional design, some 2000 Megolas were built between 1922 and the firm's closure in 1925.

■ MEGURO

Founded in 1924, Meguro was one of the earliest Japanese motorcycle manufacturers. In the 1930s the firm's main bike was the 500cc Z97, a copy of the Velocette MSS. Meguro expanded to build twins in the 1950s, such as the 500cc K1, a copy of the BSA A7. But sales fell, and following a strike the firm was taken over by Kawasaki in 1960.

■ MIG

Chinese firm MIG has built an increasingly large number of bikes in recent years, many based on earlier Japanese designs. Most have been mopeds, scooters and commuter bikes, but

■ ABOVE *MIG's QJ100 roadster is typical of the many small bikes built by Chinese firms in recent years.*

MIG did build a version of Honda's CB500-four of the 1970s.

■ MONTESA

Spain's first major bike manufacturer was founded in 1944 by Francisco Bulto, who

■ LEFT *The 640cc Megola engine of 1922 featured five cylinders arranged radially inside the front wheel.*

■ BELOW *Despite its feet-forward position, this 14bhp Megola racer won the German championship in 1922.*

later left to form Bultaco, and Pedro Perm-anyer. Early bikes included successful two-stroke road racers and the Impala roadster. In recent years the Barcelona firm has been best known for trials, winning the world championship in 1980 and producing the long-running Cota model. Financial problems in the 1980s led to an association with Honda, whose engines have been used by Montesa in recent years.

■ MONTGOMERY

Founded in 1902, Montgomery built a wide variety of bikes using bought-in engines ranging from 150cc Villiers two-strokes to 1000cc JAPs. A typical mid-1930s bike was the Greyhound, a 500cc JAP-powered single capable of 75mph (120kph). It was well-made but expensive, and Montgomery did not resume production after the Second World War.

the triumphant 1957 season Mondial, who could not sell enough roadsters to finance the racing team, quit the sport. Two of the 250s were sold to Mike Hailwood, who won many races on them in Britain. In the 1960s Mondial made a partially successful return to racing using two-stroke engines. In 1992 the Mondial name resurfaced again, in the shape of a KTM-engined 560cc single-cylinder racebike produced by Pierluigi Boselli, son of the firm's former owner.

■ ABOVE *Mondial won a hat-trick of 125cc world titles with twin-cam singles similar to this 1949 machine.*

■ ABOVE *Former champion Cecil Sandford revived memories on a "dustbin-faired" 125cc at a Monza classic event.*

MOTO GUZZI

■ MOTO GUZZI FALCONE

Italy's largest motorcycle manufacturer for much of its long history, Guzzi dates back to the closing years of the First World War when three air corps friends, Carlo Guzzi, Giorgio Parodi and Giovanni Ravelli, planned a bike firm. After Ravelli was killed in a flying crash, the other two adopted the air corps' eagle symbol in his honour. In 1920 Carlo Guzzi designed the firm's first bike, a 500cc four-stroke with a single, horizontal cylinder. The Normale model was released two years later and, boosted by racing success, rapidly became popular.

Guzzi retained and updated the 500cc flat-single format for many years, leaving many of its more adventurous engine layouts for racing. Landmark singles included the GT luxury tourer of 1928, with its novel sprung frame, and the Sport 15 of 1931, finished in the bright red that became a favourite

■ ABOVE *Founding partner Carlo Guzzi designed the road and race bikes that made Guzzi a leading marque in the 1920s.*

■ LEFT *Fergus Anderson riding his works Falcone on the way to victory in the 250cc Lightweight TT in 1952.*

MOTO GUZZI FALCONE (1950)

Engine	Aircooled 2-valve OHV pushrod single
Capacity	498cc (88 x 82mm)
Power	23bhp @ 4500rpm
Weight	170kg (374lb) dry
Top speed	85mph (136kph)

■ ABOVE *Guzzi's decision to quit racing in 1957 meant the exotic and super-fast V-eight never won a Grand Prix.*

■ LEFT *The quick and practical 250cc Airone, launched in 1939, was still popular when this bike was built in 1953.*

Sport and Touring forms. Further updates kept it in production until 1976.

Guzzi's horizontal singles were hugely successful in racing, winning three 250cc world titles between 1949 and 1952, and then being enlarged to 350cc to take five consecutive championships from 1953. The first two championships were won by Scottish ace Fergus Anderson, who then took over as Guzzi's competition manager.

The greatest machine of all was the legendary 500cc V-eight, which was designed by Giulio Carcano and first raced in 1956. The watercooled, quad-cam, 90-degree V-eight revved to 12,000rpm, produced 72bhp and was timed at a phenomenal 178mph (286kph) at the Belgian GP in 1957. Despite these feats, Guzzi unfortunately pulled out of Grand Prix racing at the end of that season, so the V-eight never really fulfilled its true potential.

Guzzi colour. The colour was also used for the famous series of production racers, which began in 1938 with the 28bhp, 100mph (160kph) Condor, and continued with the Dondolino, Gambalunga and the 250cc Albatros – all of which won at the highest level.

The best loved road-going single was the Falcone, which was introduced in 1950 showing clear links with the Normale of almost three decades earlier. Essentially a sports version of the previous year's Astore tourer, the Falcone featured flat handlebars and rearset footrests.

In standard trim its top speed was 85mph (136kph), but when tuned with Dondolino engine parts the Falcone was good for over 100mph (160kph) which, along with the lazy, low revving power delivery, helped to explain its popularity. From 1953 the Falcone was built in

OTHER MAKES

■ MORBIDELLI

Self-made businessman and fanatical motorcyclist Giancarlo Morbidelli used his huge woodwork machinery firm to finance production of some superb race-bikes. Morbidellis won three consecutive 125cc world titles in the mid-1970s, plus

the 250cc crown in 1977. Another 125cc title was added the following year, after the MBA firm had been created to produce replicas, and the two-stroke twins remained competitive for several more years. A four-cylinder 500cc racer proved less successful, and Giancarlo Morbidelli finally quit racing. In 1994, he returned to motorcycling with a prototype roadster – an exotic sports-tourer – powered by a purpose-built, 850cc watercooled V-eight engine.

■ LEFT *Morbidelli's V-eight prototype featured controversial styling by leading car-design studio Pininfarina.*

MOTO GUZZI

■ MOTO GUZZI LE MANS 850

Guzzi's trademark transverse 90-degree V-twin engine design was first seen in an unusual 754cc three-wheeled mountain vehicle called the 3 x 3, built in small numbers for the Italian ministry of defence between 1960 and 1963. In 1964 Guzzi revised the engine for a military bike, and realized the machine had potential for civilian use too.

The V7 went into production in 1967, and two years later was followed by the V7 Special, whose 757cc engine produced 45bhp. With its shaft final drive, the Special was a practical machine whose smooth, 110mph (177kph) performance and stable

■ RIGHT *Fine handling combined with the Le Mans' power and smoothness to make a formidable Superbike.*

■ BELOW *The Le Mans Mk.1's tiny fly-screen added the finishing touch to the Guzzi's classically elegant profile.*

■ FAR LEFT
The protruding cylinders of Guzzi's traditional V-twin were tuned to excellent effect for the Le Mans.

■ LEFT *Guzzi's big factory at Mandello del Lario has run at well below full capacity in recent years.*

MOTO GUZZI 850 LE MANS MK.1 (1976)

Engine	Aircooled 4-valve OHV pushrod 90-degree transverse V-twin
Capacity	844cc (83 x 78mm)
Power	71bhp @ 7300rpm
Weight	215kg (473lb) dry
Top speed	130mph (209kph)

handling did much to establish Guzzi in the large-capacity market. In 1972 Guzzi released its first genuine high-performance V-twin, the V7 Sport. It featured a reworked 748cc motor and a lower frame that gave 125mph (201kph) performance with excellent handling.

Four years later came the most famous model of all – the 850 Le Mans. This lean sportster, with its neat headlamp fairing and striking, angular seat, was powered by a tuned version of the existing 844cc motor. High-compression pistons, big valves and unfiltered 36mm Dell'Orto carburettors helped raise peak output to 71bhp, which gave a top speed of 130mph (209kph). The shaft-drive motor's long-legged power delivery, coupled with good handling and excellent braking – using Guzzi's new system, which linked the front and rear discs – made the Le Mans one of the finest superbikes of the 1970s.

Times have often been difficult at Guzzi since the firm's great days in the early 1960s, when the big, modern factory at Mandello del Lario, on Lake

Lecco, employed over 1500 people, and boasted its own hydro-electric power stations and an advanced wind-tunnel. By the mid-1960s, factors including the changing bike market, the retirement of the firm's founders and a misguided move into moped production had left Guzzi in serious financial trouble. In 1966 the company went into receivership, reopening a year later with a new owner. In 1973 Guzzi was bought by Alejandro De Tomaso, the Argentinian car baron, who maintained control for the next two decades without providing the investment that many enthusiasts had hoped for.

Guzzi's best-selling model for much of that time was the California, which was initially produced in 1971 as an American market version of the V7 Special, complete with higher bars, "buddy" seat and standard-fitment

screen and panniers. Over the years the California has seen several restyles and revisions, notably in its engine capacity which has grown to 850, 950 and finally 1100cc. In 1994 the California's aircooled, pushrod V-twin engine was fitted with optional fuel-injection, making an even more sophisticated and practical motorcycle tourer.

■ ABOVE *The 750cc V7 Special of 1969 was the basis for Guzzi's long-running range of V-twin tourers.*

■ LEFT *In 1994 the California tourer, its capacity by now 1100cc, was offered with optional fuel-injection.*

■ BELOW *Inspiration for the Daytona came from American "Dr John" Wittner's highly successful racing Guzzis.*

■ BOTTOM *The Daytona's sleek styling, updated V-twin engine and race-bred chassis made an impressive combination.*

MOTO GUZZI

■ MOTO GUZZI DAYTONA 1000

Guzzi took a long time to produce a fitting successor to the original Le Mans, which was gradually developed through the 1980s while becoming decreasingly competitive. Finally, in 1992, came a new generation sportsbike, the Daytona 1000. Its design owed much to "Dr John" Wittner, an American dentist-turned-engineer who had achieved much success with Guzzi-powered racebikes in the late 1980s before coming to work at Mandello.

The roadster's chassis, consisting of a steel spine frame and single-shock rear suspension – incorporating a linkage to counteract the shaft drive's adverse

MOTO GUZZI DAYTONA 1000 (1992)

Engine	Aircooled 8-valve high-cam 90-degree transverse V-twin
Capacity	992cc (90 x 78mm)
Power	95bhp @ 8000rpm
Weight	205kg (451lb) dry
Top speed	150mph (241kph)

affect on handling – was developed from the one on Wittner's racebikes. It held a revised 992cc version of the aircooled V-twin, with fuel-injection, four valves per cylinder and a high camshaft design in place of the old engine's pushrod-operated layout. The handsome, 95bhp Daytona combined a 150mph (241kph) top speed with good handling plus Guzzi's traditional long-legged feel. Along with the cheaper, carburetted 1100 Sport that followed in 1994, the Daytona proved there was still sporting life in Guzzi's V-twin format.

OTHER MAKES

■ MOTO MARTIN

Frenchman Georges Martin was one of the leading chassis specialists of the 1970s and early 1980s, producing stable-handling and beautifully styled café racers typically based on four-cylinder motors such as Kawasaki's Z1000 and Suzuki's GSX1100. Arguably the best of all was the Martin CBX1000, which was powered by a tuned version of Honda's six-cylinder engine.

■ ABOVE *The Martin CBX1000 was one of the fastest and most aggressively styled specials of the early 1980s.*

■ MOTO MORINI

Alfonso Morini began building bikes in partnership with Mario Mezzetti, under the MM name in the 1920s, and rode one himself to a class win in the 1927 Italian Grand Prix at Monza. After setting up under his own name after the War, Morini built roadsters and successful racers, most notably the superb DOHC 250 on which Tarquinio Provini was runner up in the 1963 world championship. The Bologna firm's best known roadster was the handsome and

■ ABOVE *Morini's pretty and fine-handling 3¹/₂ Sport was great fun on twisty roads, and despite the V-twin's modest power even made a useful racer.*

very quick 344cc 3¹/₂ Sport of the mid-1970s. Cagiva bought Morini in 1987, since when the name has been little used.

■ MOTOSACOCHE

Swiss brothers Henri and Armand Dufaux began by making a successful 215cc motorized bicycle in 1900, and by the 1920s had progressed to building 350 and 500cc four-stroke singles that gained many race wins and speed records. When sales fell in the 1930s, Motosacoche left bike production to concentrate on industrial engines.

■ MOTOTRANS

After being founded in 1957 to produce Ducati singles under licence, Spanish firm Mototrans became a manufacturer in its own right. Models included the Yak 410 trail bike plus some Zündapp-powered lightweights that were built in 1982, shortly before the factory was taken over and closed by Yamaha.

■ MÜNCH

The car-engined monster-bikes produced by German engineer Friedel Münch since 1966 have been some of the biggest and most expensive on two wheels. The first Münch Mammut models were powered by an aircooled, 1000cc four-cylinder NSU car engine, held in a huge chassis based on a twin-shock, tubular steel frame. By the early 1990s almost 500 had been built, later models with capacity of up to 1996cc and weight of over 350kg. The most recent Münch, the turbocharged Titan 2000, produced 150bhp and featured a hydraulic centre-stand.

■ ABOVE *The mighty Münch Mammut – or Mammoth – was one of the biggest, most powerful and most expensive superbikes of the 1970s.*

MV AGUSTA

■ MV AGUSTA 500cc FOUR

There is no greater name in motorcycle racing than MV Agusta, whose record of 17 consecutive world 500cc championships between 1958 and 1974 will probably never be equalled. In all, the

MV AGUSTA 500cc FOUR (1956)	
Engine	Aircooled 8-valve DOHC transverse four
Capacity	498cc (53 x 56.4mm)
Power	70bhp @ 10,500rpm
Weight	140kg (308lb) dry
Top speed	155mph (249kph)

small factory from Gallarate won 38 riders' world titles, 37 manufacturers' championships and over 3000 international races, as well as building the mighty four-cylinder roadsters that were arguably the fastest and most glamorous superbikes of the 1970s.

The Meccanica Verghera motorcycle firm was founded in the village of Verghera towards the end of the Second World War by Count Domenico Agusta, the eldest of four brothers whose late father, a Sicilian aristocrat, had been a noted aviation pioneer. Domenico turned to bikes, and in 1945 released a 98cc two-stroke that sold well and was also raced with instant success. Pure racers as well as other roadsters followed, and

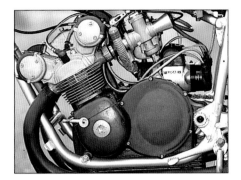

■ LEFT *The Agusta firm's gear-cog logo became synonymous with success.*

■ RIGHT *Count Domenico Agusta strikes a pose with team riders John Surtees, Umberto Masetti, Carlo Ubbiali, Carlo Bandirola, Angelo Copeta, Remo Venturi, Luigi Taveri and Tito Forconi in 1956.*

in 1952 Englishman Cecil Sandford won MV's first world title in the 125cc class. In the smaller Grand Prix categories the firm's star rider was Italian ace Carlo Ubbiali, who won five 125cc championships for MV between 1955 and 1960, plus three more on a 250.

But it was in the bigger classes that MV was most successful. The design of MV's first twin-cam 500cc four of 1950 owed much to Gilera, for whom both chief engineer Piero Remor and team manager Arturo Magni had worked. Early bikes featured shaft final drive and a gearlever on each side of the engine, but after poor results a more conventional layout was adopted. John Surtees won MV's first 500cc championship in 1956 and went on to take three more, often winning with ease after the rival factories' withdrawal from racing in 1957. Gary Hocking and Mike Hailwood continued the run, then Giacomo Agostini took over with seven straight championships between 1966 and 1971, using a fine-handling three-cylinder machine.

MV had little serious opposition for long periods during the 1960s, but the so-called "Gallarate fire engines" were increasingly tested by the Japanese two-stroke challenge in the early 1970s. New four-valves-per-cylinder fours were built for both the 350 and 500cc classes, the smaller bike allowing Agostini to win his sixth consecutive 350cc title in 1973. Phil Read used the new 500, which produced 102bhp at 14,000rpm, to take the championship in 1973 and 1974, averaging 130mph (209kph) in winning the Belgian Grand Prix. Ironically it was Agostini, now on a two-stroke Yamaha, who finally ended the Italian firm's domination in 1975.

■ LEFT *Giacomo Agostini, who won 14 world titles for MV, takes "Ago's leap" en route to victory in the 1970 Senior TT.*

■ BELOW *This SOHC, single-cylinder racer, built by MV in the mid-1950s, was capable of over 90mph (145kph).*

MV AGUSTA

■ LEFT *The best-handling MV fours were specials with frames built by former race team boss Arturo Magni.*

■ MV AGUSTA 750 SPORT

Despite producing many successful small-capacity roadsters throughout the 1950s and 1960s – bikes with names like the Pullman, the Turismo Rapido and the Raid – MV was slow to capitalize on its racing success with a four-cylinder street bike. Even when a DOHC MV four did reach the road in 1966 it was not a race-replica but an

■ BELOW *With blue, white and red finish and its mighty engine on show, the 750 Sport of 1973 was a handsome bike.*

ugly, hump-tanked 600cc shaft-drive tourer designed at the insistence of the firm's autocratic owner Domenico Agusta, who did not want the production bike to be raced, for fear of devaluing his factory team's hard-won reputation.

The expensive 600 Four was a flop, and in 1970 MV belatedly released a much racier and more exciting roadster called the 750 Sport. This was all that

MV's racing fans had dreamt of. The big, four-cylinder engine had gear drive to twin overhead cams and produced 69bhp. The racy chassis featured clip-on handlebars, a sculpted fuel tank, humped seat and huge Grimeca four-leading-shoe front brake. The Sport was beautiful, expensive and fast, though its 120mph (192kph) top speed did not match MV's claims. Despite too much

MV AGUSTA 750 SPORT (1973)	
Engine	Aircooled 8-valve DOHC transverse four
Capacity	743cc (65 x 56mm)
Power	69bhp @ 7900rpm
Weight	230kg (506lb) dry
Top speed	120mph (192kph)

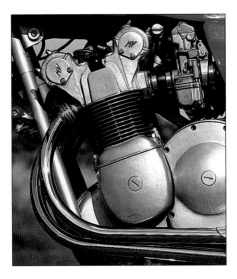

■ LEFT *MV's race-derived four, with gear drive to twin cams, was powerful but very expensive to produce.*

■ RIGHT *The last four-cylinder MV was the 750S America of 1975, here fitted with a handlebar fairing.*

weight and the retained shaft drive it handled reasonably well, and the howl from its four shiny megaphone exhausts was gloriously evocative of the Gallarate bikes that still dominated Grand Prix racing.

In subsequent years the Sport was updated with disc brakes, more power and a full fairing. And in 1975 came the 750S America, built for the US market with new, angular styling and a 789cc, 75bhp engine that pushed its top speed towards 130mph (209kph). Like the Sport, the America was an exotic and hugely desirable superbike, but it was no more commercially successful than its predecessor. Glamorous as the fours were, their intricate, competition-derived engine design and low-volume, hand-built construction meant that MVs were not profitable even at the huge

■ RIGHT *Its rarity has made MV's ugly 600cc tourer hugely valuable, but it was a sales disaster back in 1966.*

prices they commanded.

Far from making money for MV, the big roadsters merely added to the firm's problems. Domenico Agusta had died of a heart attack in 1971. His brother Corradino, who had taken over, could not match the passion with which Domenico had run MV's motorcycle division, by then a loss-making part of

the Agusta helicopter firm. By 1977 the Agusta family had lost control of much of the MV business, and was powerless to prevent motorcycle production being halted. Bikes remained on sale until stocks ran out, and in early 1980 MV closed. The name was bought by Cagiva, who could be planning MV's comeback with a three-cylinder Superbike.

■ RIGHT *MV's roadster production in the 1950s was based on small, sporty bikes such as the 175 CSS known as the "Disco Volante" (Flying Saucer) due to the unusual shape of its fuel tank.*

MuZ

■ MuZ SKORPION SPORT

The original company, MZ, was founded after the Second World War at the former DKW factory at Zschopau in East Germany, after former DKW personnel had relocated in the West. The firm was

MuZ SKORPION SPORT (1994)	
Engine	Aircooled 2-valve SOHC single
Capacity	660cc (100 x 84mm)
Power	48bhp @ 6500rpm
Weight	174kg (383lb) dry
Top speed	105mph (168kph)

very successful in off-road competition in the 1960s, winning a string of honours in the International Six Days Enduro. But it was in road racing that MZ had the biggest impact, due to the powerful two-strokes developed by their engineer Walter Kaaden. Star rider Ernst Degner was on the verge of winning the 125cc world championship in 1961 when he defected, taking MZ's

secrets to Suzuki. Degner ended up second that year, and MZ never won the title.

Until quite recently, MZ's roadsters were predominantly single-cylinder two-strokes of moderate performance and curious, old-fashioned styling. Bikes such as the ES250/2 Trophy and TS250/1 Supa Five of the 1970s, and the later but only slightly better looking

■ LEFT *The former MZ firm had a strong tradition in off-road events such as the International Six Days Enduro.*

■ BELOW *MZ roadsters such as the 250cc Supa Five were popular for their price and practicality, but not their looks.*

■ BELOW *Ernst Degner (right), who later went to Suzuki, discusses two-stroke tuning with Walter Kaaden.*

ETZ250, provided cheap, reliable motorcycling for large numbers of riders, mainly in Eastern Europe.

After German reunification MZ fell into financial trouble, but resurfaced in 1994 with new management, a new name – MuZ – and a stylish new single-cylinder roadster, the Skorpion. Designed by British consultants Seymour Powell and powered by the aircooled, four-stroke engine from Yamaha's XTZ660 trail bike, the Skorpion was a neat and reasonably quick roadster, with a 105mph (168kph) top speed and good handling. Although MuZ remained in a difficult financial position, the Skorpion's arrival gave hope for a more prosperous future.

OTHER MAKES

■ NER-A-CAR

The name of this unusually designed machine of the 1920s was doubly apt, because it was designed by an American called Carl Neracher with the intention of being a bike that was as near a car as possible. His long, low creation was built first in Syracuse, New York state and then in Britain, initially with a 221cc two-stroke engine and later with a 350cc four-stroke single. Although civilized and very stable, thanks partly to its innovative hub-centre steering, the Ner-a-Car was not a commercial success. Production began in 1921 at the improbably high rate of 150 per day, and lasted only until 1926.

■ ABOVE *The Ner-a-Car was stable and civilized, but even in the 1920s most riders preferred sportier bikes.*

■ ABOVE *New Imperial's fast and handsome 500cc V-twin set records and won many races in the mid-1930s.*

■ NEW IMPERIAL

Birmingham firm New Imperial was notable in the early 1930s for pioneering unit construction of engine and gearbox on bikes including the Unit Minor 150 and Unit Super 250. Sporting successes included Ginger Wood's 102.2mph (164.4kph) average for an hour at Brooklands in 1934 on a 500cc V-twin, and Bob Foster's win in the 1936 Lightweight TT. The factory was bought by Jack Sangster, owner of Ariel and Triumph, and production did not restart after the Second World War.

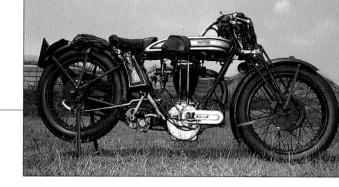

■ LEFT *This Model 19, from 1926, was finished in Norton's silver-and-black colours.*

NORTON

■ NORTON CS1

James Lansdowne Norton built his first motorcycle in 1902, and soon gained a reputation for rapid racing bikes and strong, reliable roadsters. In 1907 Rem Fowler used a Peugeot-engined Norton to win the twin-cylinder class of the first Isle of Man TT. A year later, Norton introduced both single and twin-cylinder engines of its own construction. Early models included the 490cc 16H, a high-performance roadster, and the 633cc long-stroke Big 4, which was named after its 4bhp rating and was popular for pulling sidecars. But James Norton was a better engineer than businessman, and the firm went into liquidation in 1913.

Norton Motors Ltd was formed shortly afterwards under joint directorship of

■ LEFT *The right of the CS1's engine shows the bevel-driven overhead cam that gave the CamShaft 1 its name.*

■ BELOW *This 1927 works CS1 is pictured at Brooklands.*

NORTON CS1 (1927)

Engine	Aircooled 2-valve SOHC single
Capacity	490cc (79 x 100mm)
Power	20bhp approx
Weight	145kg (319lb) wet
Top speed	80mph (128kph)

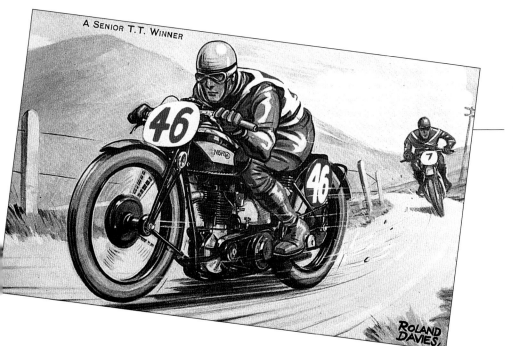

A SENIOR T.T. WINNER

ROLAND DAVIES

■ ABOVE *This scene of a victorious Norton from the early 1930s celebrates the firm's long run of wins in the Senior TT.*

■ LEFT *Norton's key figures James "Pa" Norton and tuner "Wizard" O'Donovan, pose with rider Rex Judd.*

OTHER MAKES

■ NIMBUS

Throughout its existence from 1919 to closure in the late 1950s, Danish firm Nimbus concentrated solely on bikes with a 750cc, aircooled in-line four-cylinder engine and shaft final drive. Early models had inlet-over-exhaust valve operation; later bikes used a redesigned, SOHC motor producing 22bhp. Nimbus's military fours were much-used by the Danish armed forces, but the civilian models were not exported in great numbers.

■ ABOVE *The 1934 Nimbus was one of the first to use the Danish firm's new SOHC in-line-four engine, which was introduced in that year.*

■ NORMAN

In the 1950s Norman, a small firm from Kent, was as notable for its displays at London's annual bike show as for its modest range of small capacity two-strokes. Villiers-engined roadsters such as the TS Uni-Twin and the B3 were competent and reliable, but performance was only moderate and the factory was closed in 1962.

■ ABOVE *One of Norman's last and best roadsters was the B4 Sports of 1961, powered by a 250cc, twin-cylinder Villiers two-stroke engine.*

James Norton and Bob Shelley, whose brother-in-law Dan "Wizard" O'Donovan was a top racer and tuner. Based at Brooklands, O'Donovan developed the 490cc Norton single to produce the Brooklands Special or BS, which was sold with a certificate confirming that it had exceeded 75mph (120kph) at the Surrey track. The BS was the world's first production racing bike, and was also built in Brooklands Road Special (BRS) form, timed at 70mph (112kph). The chassis that O'Donovan used to test the BS and BRS engines at Brooklands was later restored, became known as "Old Miracle", and was ridden in classic events for many years.

In the early 1920s Norton converted the single-cylinder engine to overhead valve operation, producing the Model 18 roadster. The PHV single won the Senior TT in 1924, a year before "Pa" Norton died, aged 56, following a long-standing heart problem. In 1927 the firm from Bracebridge Street, Birmingham introduced another technical advance with the CS1, which featured an overhead camshaft. The CS1 was immediately successful in racing, being ridden to victory by the great Stanley Woods and others, and a year later was released as a super-sports roadster.

■ BELOW *The McCandless brothers' Featherbed frame gave the Manx, pictured here in 1955, superb handling.*

■ BOTTOM *Classically simple, its lasting success made the Manx the definitive British racing single.*

NORTON

■ NORTON 500cc MANX

The 1930s were great years for Norton, who won every Senior and Junior TT race but two between 1931 and 1938. Led by team manager, tuner and former rider Joe Craig, the firm more than lived up to the "Unapproachable Norton" slogan that had been coined years earlier. Norton's sporting single during the 1930s was the International. The firm's Isle of Man success led to the racing version of this model, produced to individual orders at Norton's Bracebridge Street factory, being given the name Manx.

The most famous version of the Manx was created in 1950, when the works racebike, which had used a twin-camshaft engine since 1937, was

redesigned using an innovative tubular steel chassis devised by Irish racing brothers Rex and Cromie McCandless. During testing at Silverstone, Norton works rider Harold Daniell inadvertently christened the frame with his comment that the new bike felt as though he was riding a feather bed. Geoff Duke went on

to win both 500 and 350cc world titles on the fine-handling Featherbed Manx in 1951, retaining the 350 championship in 1952.

Although it was eventually overcome by the more powerful four-cylinder 500s of Gilera and MV Agusta, the Manx took numerous famous victories in

NORTON 500cc MANX (1962)	
Engine	Aircooled 4-valve DOHC single
Capacity	498cc (86 x 85.8mm)
Power	54bhp @ 7200rpm
Weight	140kg (308lb) dry
Top speed	140mph (225kph)

■ BELOW *The Dominator 99, introduced in 1956, provided 100mph (160kph) top speed and good handling.*

subsequent years, many by private riders on production bikes after Norton's factory team had been disbanded in 1955. A Manx ridden by Godfrey Nash won the Yugoslavian Grand Prix as late as 1969, and in the 1980s the single found a new lease of life with the rise in popularity of classic racing.

The success of Triumph's Speed Twin and its derivatives led Norton to introduce its own parallel twin, the 500cc Model 7 Dominator, in 1949. Designed by Bert Hopwood, the Dominator produced 29bhp, managed about 90mph (145kph), was reliable and handled well, though the initial model's brakes were poor. In 1952 Norton combined the twin-cylinder powerplant with the Featherbed frame made famous by the Manx single, to produce the Dominator 88. This was the bike that first earned the reputation for fine handling that Norton twins retained for many years.

The first Norton twin whose engine truly matched its chassis was the Dominator 650SS, which was launched in 1962 with an uprated, 49bhp motor in a Featherbed frame. With paintwork in

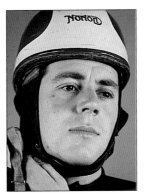

■ LEFT *A 600cc parallel-twin engine and Featherbed frame made the "Dommie 99" a winner.*

■ FAR LEFT *Geoff Duke won three world championships on Norton's factory singles.*

Norton's traditional silver the 650SS was a handsome bike, and it was fast, torquey and stable too. But the 650SS and later 750cc Atlas did not sell particularly well, partly due to relatively low production levels and high prices. That did not help the always difficult financial situation at Norton. In 1953 the firm had been bought by AMC, owners of AJS and Matchless, and in 1963 production was moved to AMC's factory in south London.

■ LEFT *Among the best Norton twins was the powerful and stylish 650SS, pictured here in 1966 form.*

NORTON

■ LEFT *Its blend of smoothness and traditional Norton handling made the Commando ideal for hard riding.*

■ BELOW *The Commando motor's vibration was controlled by Norton's Isolastic mounting system.*

■ BOTTOM *The Fastback Commando was a very stylish bike.*

■ NORTON COMMANDO 750cc FASTBACK

The Norton Commando was one of the best and most famous parallel twins of them all. It was released in 1968, created massive interest – not least due to the striking styling that earned it the Fastback name – and sold well despite a backdrop of Norton's mounting financial problems. Powered by the 745cc engine from the 750 Atlas model, the Commando produced 58bhp and weighed a respectable 190kg (418lb). Its 115mph (185kph) plus performance was well-controlled by a chassis that again upheld Norton's reputation for handling and roadholding.

The Commando chassis was also notable for the way it controlled the

NORTON COMMANDO 750cc FASTBACK (1968)	
Engine	Aircooled 4-valve OHV pushrod parallel twin
Capacity	745cc (73 x 89mm)
Power	58bhp @ 6800rpm
Weight	190kg (418lb) dry
Top speed	117mph (187kph)

■ LEFT *Steve Hislop's 1992 Senior TT win on the rotary racer evoked Norton's glory years.*

■ FAR LEFT TOP *Peter Williams won the Formula 750 TT for Norton in 1973.*

■ FAR LEFT BELOW *The Classic was the first Norton rotary to go on sale to the public.*

■ BELOW *The F1 sportster (left) was inspired by Steve Spray's 1989 racebike.*

traditional big-twin vibration that had plagued the Atlas. Norton's Isolastic system was a method of attaching the angled-forward engine assembly to the twin-cradle frame via several adjustable rubber mounts, which allowed the motor to shake without upsetting the rest of the bike. The system worked, maintaining a smooth ride even when, six years later, the engine was bored out to produce the 850 Commando.

Despite lacking power compared to most of its circuit rivals, the Commando was raced with some success in the early 1970s. Norton's Formula 750 racer used an innovative steel monocoque frame that helped give advantages in weight and aerodynamics. The bike was developed and ridden by Peter Williams, who won the 1973 Formula 750 TT on it. A road-going replica was also produced, but such rearguard actions were not enough to save Norton, which by now was part of the Norton Villiers Triumph group that had been struggling for years. NVT duly went into liquidation, and the last Commandos were built in 1978.

Norton's name did not disappear altogether, however, and between 1977 and 1987 the company continued low

key development of a rotary-engined bike that was used by several British police forces. Eventually Norton, now based at Shenstone in Staffordshire, produced a limited edition civilian roadster called the Classic, powered by a 588cc twin-chamber rotary engine. The touring Commander followed, and public interest in Norton snowballed when enthusiastic workers built an alloy-framed rotary racer that won two national championships in 1989.

A race-replica sportster, the F1, followed a year later, combining good

looks with 145mph (233kph) speed and sure-footed handling. The F1, however, had some rough edges, and its low-volume production kept prices up and profits down. By the mid-1990s Norton's promising recovery had foundered, several former directors had been accused of financial irregularities, and hundreds of shareholders had lost money invested in the company. Production of rotaries was then abandoned by the new Canadian owners, and Norton's future as a motorcycle manufacturer remained in doubt.

N S U

■ NSU 250cc SUPERMAX

German firm NSU started off by producing knitting machines, before expanding to build bicycles and then, in 1901, its first motorbike. The first machines used a combination of a Swiss-made 1.5bhp

NSU SUPERMAX (1955)

Engine	Aircooled 2-valve SOHC single
Capacity	247cc (69 x 66mm)
Power	18bhp @ 6500rpm
Weight	164kg (361lb) dry
Top speed	75mph (120kph)

■ LEFT *NSU's 250cc Supermax (left) and 125cc Superfox singles shared an SOHC single-cylinder engine layout.*

■ BELOW *The Supermax was one of the most sophisticated bikes of the 1950s, but its price limited export sales.*

■ BELOW *The Supermax's fuel cap celebrated NSU's Grand Prix success.*

■ BOTTOM *Werner Haas, pictured on the superb Rennmax parallel twin, won both 250 and 125cc titles in 1953.*

Zedel engine in a bicycle frame; two years later NSU produced its own single and V-twin engines. Production grew, and in 1929 Norton's designer Walter Moore was hired to create NSU's first overhead-camshaft model. In fact, the 500SS was so similar to Norton's CS1 that Norton workers claimed NSU stood for Norton Spares Used.

NSU was one of the world's leading manufacturers before the Second World War, and afterwards introduced innovative bikes including the 250cc Max. This featured an SOHC single-cylinder engine, pressed-steel frame and leading-link forks. The Max's most famous descendent was the Supermax, introduced in 1955, which provided smooth, reliable 75mph (120kph) performance, stable handling and excellent braking. It was beautifully engineered and constructed, traditional assets which led Honda to base several bikes on NSUs. But the Supermax and its 125cc stablemate the Superfox were too expensive to sell in large numbers, and in the early 1960s NSU abandoned bikes to concentrate on car production.

OTHER MAKES

■ OK-SUPREME

After beginning volume production in 1911, Birmingham-based OK concentrated on two-strokes, notably a bike called the Junior. The firm became OK-Supreme in 1927, the year before Frank Longman scored its only TT win. Its best-known bike was the early 1930s single, built in 250 and 350cc form, that was known as the Lighthouse after the glass inspection plate in its camshaft tower. The cheap and reliable 250cc Flying Cloud was popular in the late 1930s, but the firm built only a few grass track bikes after the Second World War.

■ ABOVE *Legendary rider and tuner Bill Lacey with a record-breaking OK-Supreme on the Brooklands banking.*

■ OSSA

Founded by Manuel Giro in the late 1940s, Ossa developed a reputation for trials, enduro and trail machines, mostly with two-stroke engines. The Barcelona firm built numerous small capacity roadsters and made an impact in road racing with Santiago Herrero, who won several 250cc Grands Prix on a single-cylinder two-stroke in the late 1960s. Sadly, Herrero was killed at the Isle of Man TT in 1970, after which Ossa quit Grand Prix racing. During the 1970s the

■ ABOVE *Over's Euro Twin, powered by Yamaha's TDM850 parallel twin motor, was fast, stylish and expensive.*

firm built successful enduro bikes and the rapid twin-cylinder two-stroke Yankee 500 roadster. But industrial problems and falling sales led to closure of the factory in 1984, after which some bikes were built as Ossamotos by a workers' co-operative.

■ OVER

The small firm run by Japanese engineer Kensei Sato has built several exotic and expensive specials in recent years, many using the oval-section tubular aluminium frames that have become an Over trademark. Among the best was the Euro Twin, powered by Yamaha's TDM850 engine.

■ ABOVE *Santiago Herrero cranks Ossa's rapid 250cc single through a bend at Brands Hatch in 1969.*

NSU's 250cc Rennmax made a brief but memorable impact on Grand Prix racing in the early 1950s. The powerful Rennmax, a DOHC parallel twin with a large-diameter steel spine frame, was in a class of its own when winning the world championship for Werner Haas in

1953 and 1954. NSU retired from Grand Prix racing after that season but continued to sell single-cylinder Sportmax racers, based on the road-going Max. Hermann-Peter Müller used one to win NSU's third consecutive 250cc championship in 1955.

PANTHER

■ LEFT *For solo use the Model 100 sloper was efficient, with a top speed of 70mph (112kph) and fair handling.*

■ BELOW *A Model 100S was typically fitted with a sidecar such as this 1957 bike's Watsonian Avon single-seater.*

■ PANTHER MODEL 100S

A big single-cylinder Panther was the definitive bike for pulling a sidecar in the 1940s and 1950s, when an "outfit" was often the main means of transport for a family unable to afford a car. Although not particularly powerful, the long-stroke Panther motor produced plenty of useful low-down torque that

PANTHER MODEL 100S (1957)	
Engine	Aircooled 2-valve OHV pushrod single
Capacity	598cc (87 x 100mm)
Power	23bhp @ 5300rpm
Weight	193kg (425lb) dry
Top speed	68mph (109kph)

made it ideal for sidecar use. The Yorkshire firm, originally known as Phelon and Moore (P&M), had been building "slopers", named after their single, angled-forward cylinder, since 1904. Panther also built Villiers-engined two-strokes until the 1930s, and recommenced two-stroke production in the 1950s with models including the 324cc Model 45 Sports.

The firm's most famous sloper was the Model 100, which was strong, slow-revving and reliable. The original 598cc overhead-valve motor, with its twin exhaust ports, was introduced in 1928, and was relatively little changed by 1957 when the Model 100S Deluxe was produced. When fitted with a Watsonian sidecar it gave undramatic but efficient and fairly smooth performance. In 1960 the firm estimated that 90 per cent of Model 100s were attached to sidecars. That left Panther vulnerable when the attraction of three wheels faded, and production ended in the late 1960s.

ROYAL ENFIELD

■ ROYAL ENFIELD 750cc INTERCEPTOR

Throughout most of its long existence Royal Enfield was one of Britain's larger manufacturers, without matching either the production levels or the glamour of giants such as BSA and Triumph. The firm from Redditch, near Birmingham, began, like many others, as a bicycle

■ ABOVE *Royal Enfield's name, little heard of in more recent years, was a very familiar sight in the 1950s and 1960s.*

■ LEFT *The Interceptor went round corners well, despite being a tall bike with rather soft front forks.*

ROYAL ENFIELD INTERCEPTOR (1965)

Engine	Aircooled 4-valve OHV pushrod parallel twin
Capacity	736cc (71 x 93mm)
Power	53bhp @ 6000rpm
Weight	193kg (425lb) wet
Top speed	105mph (168kph)

manufacturer before producing its first motorcycles in 1901. By the 1930s Enfield had adopted the Bullet name for a range of 250, 350 and 500cc four-stroke singles. After the Second World War the company introduced a redesigned Bullet single that was successful on the road and in trials, and is now built in India.

Royal Enfield followed the trend for parallel twins in 1948, with a softly-tuned 500cc roadster. Five years later the engine was enlarged to 692cc to power the Meteor, the biggest parallel twin on the market. The sportier Super Meteor led in 1958 to the Constellation, which was later sold with Royal Enfield's innovative Airflow full fairing.

Biggest and best of the twins was the Interceptor, which was released in 1962 with a 736cc engine producing 53bhp. Created partly to supply the American export market's demand for cubic inches, the Interceptor combined impressive mid-range torque and reasonable smoothness with various failings one of which was a feeble front brake. In the mid-1960s Royal Enfield suffered severe financial problems. Interceptor production moved briefly to the West Country before ending in 1968.

■ LEFT *This high-handlebarred Interceptor, built for the US market in 1965, was a handsome and powerful bike.*

RUDGE

■ RUDGE 500cc ULSTER

Two bicycle firms, Rudge and Whitworth, merged to form Rudge Whitworth and produced a 3.5bhp single-cylinder motorbike in 1909. Early innovations included a spring-up stand and a hinged rear mudguard to aid wheel removal, but it was a gearing system that led to the firm's first famous model – the Rudge Multi. This used an ingenious system of

RUDGE ULSTER (1930)

Engine	Aircooled 4-valve OHV pushrod single
Capacity	499cc (85 x 88mm)
Power	30bhp approx
Weight	131kg (290lb) dry
Top speed	100mph (160kph)

■ ABOVE *Graham Walker's 1928 Ulster Grand Prix win led to Rudge's 500cc four-valve single being called the Ulster.*

■ BELOW *The Ulster had further success with Wal Handley's Senior TT win in 1930.*

pulleys to maintain the tension of the final drive belt, while allowing the rider to select from no fewer than 21 gear ratios. The Multi was a big success, winning the 1914 Senior TT and remaining in production for nine more years.

Rudge was a leading exponent of four-valve cylinder heads in the mid-1920s, producing the 500cc single on which Graham Walker – the firm's sales manager – sped to victory in the 1928 Ulster Grand Prix.

The sportiest of Rudge's three models was renamed the Ulster in recognition. It used the firm's celebrated linked braking system, whereby the foot-pedal operated both front and rear drums, with the hand lever also working the front brake. Rudge had more racing success in the 1930s, but hit financial trouble and ceased production in 1939.

SCOTT

■ LEFT *This 596cc Flying Squirrel was built in 1950, shortly before production ceased.*

■ SCOTT SQUIRREL

Alfred Scott built some of the most advanced and distinctive bikes of motorcycling's early years. In 1909 he created a 333cc two-stroke parallel twin featuring the novelties of a kick start, foot-change two-speed gearbox and telescopic front forks. Shortly afterwards Scott adopted full watercooling and enlarged the engine to 486 and 534cc, adding performance that was put to good use in 1912 and 1913, when the

two-strokes won consecutive Senior TTs. The following year saw the start of the legendary Scott Trial, held in the Yorkshire dales near the factory.

Alfred Scott left the company after the First World War to build the three-wheeled Scott Sociable car. He died in 1923, only a year after the firm introduced the Squirrel range, and expanded with a variety of capacities, and names such as Super Squirrel, Sports Squirrel and Flying Squirrel. A typical mid-1920s Squirrel was powered by a 596cc engine with a three-speed,

hand-change gearbox. With a top speed of about 70mph (112kph), good handling and unique looks and sound, the Scotts won many followers.

The Squirrels could be temperamental, however, and prices were quite high. Later models, with conventionally shaped tanks, were heavier and less competitive, and production declined in the 1930s. In 1950 the firm was bought by Birmingham-based Scott fanatic Matt Holder, who continued developing and selling Squirrel motorcycles in small numbers right up until 1978.

■ BELOW *Scott's greatest days were already over when this distinctive three-speed, 596cc twin was built in 1928.*

SCOTT SQUIRREL (1925)

Engine	Watercooled two-stroke parallel twin
Capacity	596cc (74.6 x 68.25mm)
Power	25bhp @ 5000rpm
Weight	115kg (253lb) wet
Top speed	70mph (112kph)

SUNBEAM

■ **SUNBEAM S8**

Quality and attention to detail were characteristics for which Sunbeam's early motorcycles became known, following the Wolverhampton firm's introduction of its first model, a 350cc single, in 1912. Like Sunbeam's earlier bicycles, the single had a fully-enclosed drive chain that earned it the nickname

SUNBEAM S8 (1949)

Engine	Aircooled 4-valve SOHC tandem twin
Capacity	487cc (70 x 63.5mm)
Power	26bhp @ 5800rpm
Weight	182kg (400lb) dry
Top speed	85mph (136kph)

"Little Oil Bath". The 3.5bhp single, introduced a year later, sold well, was raced successfully and established Sunbeam's colours of black with gold lining. Development engineer George Dance set several records on Sunbeams, and the single scored two Senior TT wins in the early 1920s.

Sales declined in the 1930s, and Sunbeam was sold first to AMC and then, in 1943, to BSA. After the Second World War, BSA attempted to capitalize

on Sunbeam's reputation as the gentleman's motor bicycle by building a sophisticated roadster. The S7, released in 1947, was powered by a 487cc four-stroke tandem twin engine with shaft final drive. It had a big, heavy chassis which incorporated fat balloon tyres. The S7 was underpowered, initially vibrated terribly and handled poorly. It was also one of the most expensive bikes on the market, and unsurprisingly, was not a commercial success.

■ LEFT
*Alec Bennet won
two TTs on
black-and-gold
Sunbeams similar
to this 350cc
model 2 from
1924.*

In 1949 Sunbeam introduced the uprated S7 De Luxe, and also produced a sportier version of the twin, the S8. This featured new styling, a louder exhaust system, less weight, front forks similar to those of BSA's A10, and conventional wheels and tyres. With a top speed of about 85mph (136kph) the S8 was faster, and handled better than its predecessor. But further development was minimal, sales remained low and Sunbeam production finally ground to a halt in 1956.

OTHER MAKES

■ SINGER
The most notable design from early British firm Singer was a 222cc four-stroke single-cylinder engine which, together with its fuel tank and carburettor, was housed within a wheel. Singer bought the design in 1900 and used it, both as the rear wheel of a solo and the front wheel of a tricycle, for the next few years. The company also produced more conventional bikes before giving up to concentrate on building cars after the First World War.

■ SPONDON
Named after the Derbyshire town in which it is based, chassis specialist firm Spondon Engineering was founded by Bob Stevenson and Stuart Tiller in 1969. Several early Spondons used Yamaha two-stroke racing engines such as the 125cc AS1, TZ250 and 750cc OW31. Spondon has built frames for roadsters including the Silk and Norton's F1, and produced

numerous specials powered by Japanese fours, from Suzuki's GS1000 to Kawasaki's ZZ-R1100.

■ ABOVE *Many Sun roadsters were simple, single-cylinder two-strokes such as this 197cc model from 1956.*

■ RIGHT *Norton's rotary racebike, like the later F1 roadster, featured a Spondon twin-spar aluminium frame.*

■ SUN
Typical of the numerous British firms producing modest Villiers-engined two-strokes in the 1950s, Birmingham-based company Sun had a history that included the production of a rotary disc-valve two-stroke racer in the 1920s. Later roadsters such as the 250cc Overlander twin of 1957 were remarkable for the generous weather protection they offered. That wasn't enough to make them popular though, and Sun ceased motorcycle production a few years later.

SUZUKI

■ LEFT *Suzuki entered the bike business with the Power Free, a 36cc engine that clipped to a bicycle.*

■ **SUZUKI T20 SUPER SIX**
Michio Suzuki set up a business manufacturing silk looms in 1909, and ran it until the Second World War. In 1952, problems in the silk loom industry led Suzuki to develop and sell a 36cc two-stroke engine, named the Power Free, which clipped to a bicycle frame. An improved, 60cc version called the Diamond Free followed one year later, and in May 1954 the revived Suzuki firm launched its first complete bike, a 90cc four-stroke single named the Colleda. Entered in that year's Mount Fuji hill-climb, it triumphed over 85 rivals.

Through the late 1950s and early 60s, Suzuki concentrated on small-capacity

SUZUKI T20 SUPER SIX (1966)

Engine	Aircooled two-stroke parallel twin
Capacity	247cc (54 x 54mm)
Power	29bhp @ 7500rpm
Weight	138kg (304lb) dry
Top speed	95mph (152kph)

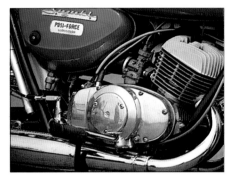

■ ABOVE *The Super Six got its name from the two-stroke parallel twin engine's six-speed gearbox.*

■ LEFT *Attractive styling combined with performance and good handling to make the Super Six popular.*

■ OPPOSITE RIGHT *The GT500 parallel twin of the early 1970s combined 110mph (177kph) top speed with only mediocre handling.*

■ OPPOSITE LEFT *Suzuki's first complete bikes were the 90 and 125cc Colleda two-strokes of the mid-1950s.*

■ RIGHT *Although it was too big and heavy to handle really well, the GT750 proved a good sports-tourer.*

■ BELOW *The GT750's rather bulbous styling made little attempt to disguise its weight.*

two-strokes, in particular on the firm's first purpose-built competition machine, the 125cc Colleda RB of 1959. They included numerous cheap commuter bikes and the sportier, 250cc T10 of 1963 – the company's first export success. But it was a new generation 250 twin, the T20 Super Six – the X6 in America – that put Suzuki on the map when it was launched in 1966.

The name referred to the two-stroke's six-speed gearbox; an even more impressive – but slightly optimistic – number was the claimed top speed of 100mph (160kph). The Super Six's all-new engine produced 29bhp and incorporated a sophisticated Posi-Force lubrication system. Other classy features included Suzuki's first twin-cradle frame, which gave good handling in conjunction with light weight. True top speed was somewhere between 90 and 100mph (144-160kph) – enough anyway to make the Super Six a big hit.

In 1967, Suzuki entered the big bike market with an enlarged two-stroke parallel twin, the T500, which was known as the Titan in America and the Cobra in Britain. Although it was simple and handled rather poorly, the 46bhp T500 was reliable, economical and fast, with a top speed of 110mph (177kph). The twin remained in production for the

next ten years, gaining a disc front brake, electronic ignition, fresh styling and the name GT500 along the way.

Suzuki's first true superbike was the GT750, the big, watercooled three-cylinder two-stroke that became known as the Kettle in Britain and the Water Buffalo in America, following its introduction in 1971. The softly-tuned 738cc engine produced 67bhp, giving the triple a top speed of 115mph (185kph) to go with its generous mid-range torque. Although smooth, quiet and comfortable, the Suzuki was also big and ponderous. It couldn't match the acceleration or excitement of rivals such as Kawasaki's 750cc H1, but its all-round ability kept the GT750 popular for most of the 1970s.

SUZUKI

■ LEFT *The GS1000 combined raw power with the best handling yet from a Japanese Superbike.*

■ SUZUKI GS1000

The GS1000 was a landmark motorcycle not just for Suzuki but for the whole Japanese industry. When it was launched in 1978, the GS outperformed Kawasaki's legendary Z1, its direct rival, in almost every area. More importantly, here at last was a big four-cylinder machine whose chassis was a match for its motor. Japan had been building great powerplants for years, but the GS was the first open-class super-bike that handled really well.

The GS1000's format was conventional, closely based on that of the GS750 introduced a year earlier. The

■ BELOW *Suzuki based the GS1000's four-cylinder motor on Kawasaki's proven DOHC, eight-valve format.*

SUZUKI GS1000 (1978)

Engine	Aircooled 8-valve DOHC transverse four
Capacity	997cc (70 x 64.8mm)
Power	87bhp @ 8000rpm
Weight	242kg (532lb) dry
Top speed	135mph (216kph)

■ RIGHT *The GS1000's rather ordinary styling disguised the fact that this was an exceptional motorcycle.*

aircooled, 997cc engine used twin cams and eight valves to produce 87bhp. The chassis incorporated a rigid tubular steel frame, sophisticated, adjustable suspension parts, wide tyres and twin front disc brakes. Styling was clean and pleasant, if a bit bland.

There was certainly nothing ordinary about the Suzuki's performance, which combined fearsome acceleration with a top speed of 135mph (216 kph). Mid-range power delivery was equally strong, and the GS was comfortable and reliable too. Better still, the bike was rock-steady in a straight line, remaining stable even at cornering speeds that left most rivals wallowing in its wake. The GS1000's only failing was a certain lack of charisma. It was a hugely impressive machine that emphasized Suzuki's arrival as a leading superbike producer.

In 1977, just a year before unleashing the GS1000, Suzuki had released its first big four-cylinder bike in the shape of the GS750 – and scored an immediate success. With a maximum output of 68bhp on tap, the twin-cam GS750 whirred smoothly to over 120mph

(193kph), cruised at 90mph (144kph) and outperformed rivals such as Honda's CB750 and Yamaha's XS750. It handled acceptably, establishing a reputation that would be enhanced by future models. Fast, refined and reliable, the GS750 four represented the start of great things for Suzuki.

The 16-valve GSX1100 that replaced the 8-valve GS1000 in 1980 was an even faster and more competent bike marred by ugly, angular looks. Two years later Suzuki revamped it to produce the stunning GSX1100S Katana, whose radical combination of nose fairing, low handlebars, humped fuel tank and combined seat/sidepanels gave a superbly raw, aggressive image. The aircooled four-cylinder engine was tuned to produce 111bhp, giving the Katana – named after a Samurai warrior's ceremonial sword – a top speed of more than 140mph (225kph). Handling was excellent despite 250kg (551lb) of weight, and the Suzuki's style and speed combined with a reasonable price to make it a big success.

S U Z U K I

■ SUZUKI GSX-R750

The arrival of Suzuki's GSX-R750 in 1985 had a huge impact on the design of supersports motorcycles. This was the first true Japanese race-replica, startlingly close to being simply Suzuki's works endurance bike in road-legal form. The GSX-R was searingly fast, outrageously light and utterly singleminded. No other mass-produced four came close to matching its uniquely aggressive, race-bred image.

Every component of the GSX-R was designed for high performance and low weight. That included the 16-valve,

■ LEFT *The original GSX-R750's ultra-light chassis gave superb cornering but occasional high-speed instability.*

■ OPPOSITE *Early GSX-Rs held an oilcooled 16-valve motor in an aluminium frame.*

■ BELOW *Heavily based on Suzuki's works endurance motorcycles, the first GSX-R750 was a genuine race-replica.*

four-cylinder engine, which was oil-cooled, had a cam cover made from lightweight magnesium, and produced 100bhp at 10,500rpm. The Suzuki's aluminium frame weighed half as much as

the steel frame of the previous GSX750, and held stout 41mm diameter front forks. A racy twin-headlamp fairing, foam-backed clocks, clip-on bars and rearset footrests completed the package.

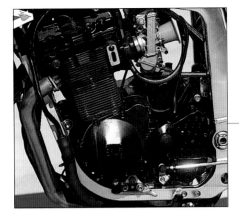

SUZUKI GSX-R750 (1985)

Engine	Oilcooled 16-valve DOHC transverse four
Capacity	749cc (70 x 48.7mm)
Power	100bhp @ 10,500rpm
Weight	176kg (387lb) dry
Top speed	145mph (233kph)

Performance lived up to all expectations. Acceleration was flat below 7000rpm, after which the GSX-R raced towards 145mph (233kph) with a muted scream from its four-into-one exhaust system. Handling and braking were exceptional, aided by the remarkably low weight of 176kg (387lb). The GSX-R750 was instantly successful both on the racetrack and in the showrooms, and its format was hastily followed by other manufacturers to create the modern brand of sporting superbike.

A year after triggering the sportsbike revolution with the GSX-R750, Suzuki produced a bigger version that brought a new dimension to two-wheeled performance. The GSX-R1100 of 1986 added mid-range power and even more outright speed to the smaller model's assets of light weight, handling and racetrack style. Its 125bhp oilcooled engine provided a 155mph (249kph) top speed, plus instant acceleration at the twist of the throttle; its lightweight aluminium-framed chassis gave unmatched open-class handling. Unfortunately for Suzuki, a 1989 redesign, the 1100K, combined fresh

■ ABOVE *Hervé Moineau led Suzuki's works endurance team to many wins.*

■ BELOW *The 1994 model GSX-R750 had a watercooled, 116bhp powerplant.*

styling with a modified chassis that ruined the big GSX-R's handling. Frequent further revamps through the 1990s restored some poise and added even more power, but the GSX-R1100 never regained its performance lead.

In contrast to its problems with the GSX-R1100, Suzuki used a process of repeated refinement to keep the GSX-R750 popular, even when its impact in racing had dimmed. The first major revision was the 750J model of 1988 – known as the Slingshot after its carburettors – which was heavier but featured new styling, uprated chassis parts and a more powerful engine. In 1992 the GSX-R gained a watercooled motor with a peak output of 116bhp, the highest yet. A stiffer frame, revised chassis geometry and upside-down forks meant that the GSX-R750W shared almost no components with the original model. It had also gained a fair amount of weight along the way. But in spirit the GSX-R750 had not changed at all.

SUZUKI

■ SUZUKI RG500

Suzuki's first move into international racing was at the Isle of Man TT in 1960, with a 125cc team including Mitsuo Itoh, who would later become the firm's racing chief. Results were modest but the experience proved vital. The team stayed at the same hotel as MZ rider Ernst Degner – who in 1961 defected from East Germany, bringing the secrets of MZ's powerful two-strokes to Suzuki. Degner won the Japanese firm's first world championship in 1962, in the new 50cc class. New Zealander Hugh Anderson and Germany's Hans-Georg Anscheidt added five more titles in the following six seasons on Suzuki's peaky little 50cc machines, and Anderson went on to win the 125cc championship in 1963 and 1965.

SUZUKI RG500 (1976)

Engine	Watercooled rotary disc-valve two-stroke square four
Capacity	495cc (54 x 54mm)
Power	114bhp @ 11,000rpm
Weight	125kg (275lb) dry
Top speed	170mph (272kph)

Success in the prestigious 500cc class was eventually achieved with the legendary square-four RG500, which not only won four world championships but was favoured by privateer racers for over a decade. The RG's layout was developed from that of the short-lived 250cc RZ63 square-four of the mid-1960s, whose habit of seizing at high speed earned it the name "Whispering Death". The RG500 was first raced in 1974 by riders including rising British star Barry Sheene. After initial problems had been solved, its watercooled, disc-valve two-stroke engine proved to be powerful and reliable.

In 1976 the RG500, redesigned with new 54 x 54mm engine dimensions and with its output increased to 114bhp at 11,000 rpm, took Sheene to his and

■ RIGHT AND
BELOW *Barry
Sheene's glamour
and showmanship
were as important
to Suzuki as his
riding ability.*

■ RIGHT *Kevin
Schwantz won the 1993
title on the RGV500.*

■ BELOW RIGHT *Schwantz won two
Grands Prix on the RGV500 in 1988, but
winning the title took another five years.*

five Grand Prix wins were matched by
five crashes that left him second in the
championship.

In 1992 Suzuki followed Honda's lead
in revising the RGV, whose cylinders
were by now spaced at 70 degrees, with
a big bang firing order that made the
170bhp V-four more rideable. Injuries
ruined that season for Schwantz, but in
1993 his matured but still aggressive
riding, coupled with the Suzuki's speed,
reliability and traditional fine handling,
finally earned the Texan the right to
replace his familiar No. 34 plate with
the champion's No. 1.

Suzuki's first 500cc championship. RG
riders also filled the next five places.
Sheene retained the title for the Heron
Suzuki team in 1977, and Italians Marco
Lucchinelli and Franco Uncini won the
championship on Team Gallina RG500s
in 1981 and 1982. By then, the engine
had become a stepped-four, producing
124bhp, and the frame tubes were
aluminium instead of the original steel.

In 1987 the RG500 was replaced by
an all-new V-four, the RGV500, and
Suzuki increased its racing involvement
with a full factory-backed team. That
season saw some promising Grand Prix
rides from young American star Kevin
Schwantz, beginning a long association
with Suzuki. The following five seasons
would ultimately prove frustrating,
particularly in 1990 when Schwantz's

TRIUMPH

■ LEFT *By 1950 the Speed Twin had telescopic forks, headlamp nacelle and a maroon finish.*

■ BELOW *Edward Turner (second left) often provided inspired leadership.*

■ BOTTOM *The original late 1930s Speed Twin was fast and light.*

■ TRIUMPH SPEED TWIN
Triumph, one of Britain's oldest and most famous manufacturers, was founded by two Germans. Siegfried Bettmann sold bicycles under his own name in the 1880s before changing his firm's name to Triumph. In 1902, in partnership with Mauritz Schulte, Bettmann fitted a Belgian 2.25bhp Minerva engine into a bicycle to produce the first Triumph motorcycle.

TRIUMPH SPEED TWIN (1937)	
Engine	Aircooled 4-valve OHV pushrod parallel twin
Capacity	498cc (63 x 80mm)
Power	29bhp @ 6000rpm
Weight	166kg (365lb) dry
Top speed	90mph (145kph)

Three years later the Coventry firm had designed and built its own 3bhp engine, and soon manufactured a range of bikes whose reliability earned the nickname "Trusty Triumph".

Triumph enhanced its reputation with the 500cc four-stroke single Model H, which was built in large numbers before, during and after the First World War. More innovative was the Model R, whose four-valve cylinder head layout, designed by Harry Ricardo, would be perfected by Honda 40 years later. Triumph's most popular bike of the 1920s was the 500cc sidevalve Model P,

which was produced at the impressive rate of 1000 per week. But the company hit financial problems and in 1936 was sold to Ariel owner Jack Sangster, who

■ LEFT *Triumph's logo was a familiar sight in the 1950s.*

■ RIGHT *Early models, like this 1912 single, inspired the nickname "Trusty Triumph".*

■ BELOW *The 650cc Thunderbird, seen here in 1956 form, was another big hit for Triumph.*

appointed 35-year-old Edward Turner as chief designer and general manager.

Turner quickly showed an inspired touch, revamping Triumph's slow-selling line of 250, 350 and 500cc singles with better finish, extra performance and new names – Tiger 70, 80 and 90. They were immediately successful, and were followed in 1937 by Turner's master-piece, the 500cc Speed Twin. This was an all-new parallel twin, a brave move considering that singles had dominated the market for several decades, and that Triumph's own 650cc Model 6/1 of four years earlier had sold poorly.

The Speed Twin produced 29bhp, had lively acceleration and a respectable top speed of 90mph (145kph), and was far smoother than most comparable singles. It was also neatly styled and compact, as the motor slotted into the familiar Tiger 90 frame. At 166kg (365lb) it was slightly lighter than the single, and was only slightly more expensive. The Speed Twin was an immediate success, marking a turning point in Triumph's fortunes and inspiring the rival manufacturers to build parallel twins of their own.

A year after the Speed Twin, in 1938, Triumph released the Tiger 100 – a sportier, 33bhp version that on a good day really was capable of touching the magic 100mph (160kph). Both models were revised slightly and continued to sell well after the Second World War. In 1950, largely to satisfy the important American export market, Triumph enlarged the engine to 650cc to produce the 6T Thunderbird. The "T-bird" was another success, its handling and acceleration more than satisfying the demands of a speed-hungry motor-cycling fraternity.

TRIUMPH

■ TRIUMPH T120 BONNEVILLE

The most famous Triumph of all was the Bonneville, which was released as a sporty 650cc twin in 1959. The original T120 Bonneville was basically the existing Tiger 110, fitted with optional splayed inlet ports and twin Amal carburettors. Its name came from the Bonneville salt flats in Utah, where a

■ LEFT *Despite marginal high-speed handling, the T120R Bonneville was one of the fastest bikes on the road in 1961.*

■ BOTTOM *This neat 650cc Bonnie was built in 1970, the year before the oil-in-frame chassis was introduced.*

TRIUMPH T120 BONNEVILLE (1961)

Engine	Aircooled 4-valve OHV pushrod parallel twin
Capacity	649cc (71 x 82mm)
Power	46bhp @ 6500rpm
Weight	183kg (403lb) dry
Top speed	110mph (177kph)

streamlined Triumph ridden by Johnny Allen had been timed at 214mph (344kph) in 1956. Although the FIM refused to ratify the speed as a world record, on a technicality, the ensuing row gave Triumph valuable publicity.

Initially the Bonneville was styled like the Tiger with a headlamp nacelle, swept-back touring handlebars and heavy mudguards. Peak output was 46bhp at 6500rpm, which was too much for the wobble-prone original chassis. In 1960 the T120 was revamped with a

new twin-cradle frame and forks, a separate headlamp, a new seat and sportier mudguards. Combining genuine 110mph (177kph) performance with mid-range punch, reasonable smoothness, adequate handling and good looks, the resultant "Bonnie" was a popular roadburner.

The Bonneville was regularly updated over the next decade, notably with the adoption of a unit-construction engine and gearbox in 1963. In 1971 the twin gained a new oil-in-frame chassis, which was much criticized until lowered a year

■ BELOW *Its 649cc, pushrod-operated parallel twin engine kept the Bonneville on top throughout the 1960s.*

■ ABOVE *The tuned Thruxton Bonneville was named after the British circuit where the T120 scored many production wins.*

■ LEFT *In 1977 Triumph produced the limited edition Silver Jubilee Bonneville.*

later. By 1972, it was estimated that 250,000 Bonnevilles had been built. Many were raced with success. In the Isle of Man, John Hartle won the production TT in 1967, and Malcolm Uphill set the first production 100mph (160kph) lap two years later.

In 1973 Triumph increased capacity to 744cc to produce the T140 Bonneville, which was more flexible, if no faster and less smooth. But parent company Norton Villiers Triumph was losing money, and rumours of imminent closure of the Meriden factory led to an 18-month sit-in, after which production was restarted by a workers' co-operative. Triumph struggled on, and fortunes improved enough to allow introduction of electric-start and eight-valve variations of the twin in the early 1980s. But low sales and rising debts finally led to the company going into liquidation in 1983, after which it was bought by current owner John Bloor. The Bonneville's final fling came when it was built under licence in Devon, by parts specialist Racing Spares, between 1985 and 1988.

OTHER MAKES

■ TRITON

The archetypal special of the 1960s was the Triton, the blend of parallel twin Triumph engine and Norton Featherbed frame that was loved by rockers and café racers. The man who did most to make the model famous was Dave Degens, the London-based racer/engineer who won the Barcelona 24-hour endurance race on one in 1970. Degens' firm, Dresda Engineering, built numerous Tritons in the 1960s, and was still producing near-identical machines 30 years later. A less common Triumph derivative was the Tribsa, which combined a similar powerplant with a BSA frame.

■ LEFT *A Dresda Triton built by racer/engineer Dave Degens was one of the ultimate café racers of the 1960s.*

TRIUMPH

■ LEFT *Despite superior handling, the T150 did not make the same impact as Honda's CB750 four.*

■ TRIUMPH T150 TRIDENT

Triumph's T150 Trident was arguably the world's finest roadster when it was released in 1969. The new 740cc, pushrod-operated three-cylinder engine produced a healthy 58bhp, sending the Trident racing to a top speed of 125mph (201kph) with a pleasant howl from its distinctively shaped ray-gun tailpipes. The Trident's unusual, angular styling was by no means to every rider's taste in 1969. But the triple was smooth, allowing relaxed 90mph (145kph) cruising for as long as the upright riding position and poor fuel economy would allow. Handling was good, too, thanks to

a modified version of the chassis used by Triumph's twins.

BSA had owned Triumph since 1951, and also built a version of the triple, the Rocket 3. This had similar styling, with the motor tilted forward in a single-downtube frame. But the struggling firm had taken too long to produce the

■ BELOW *The original Trident's angular styling was unpopular with many riders, particularly in America.*

triples, which had been under development for several years. Only a few months later, Honda released the four-cylinder CB750, with the added sophistication of an overhead-cam engine, electric starter and superior reliability. Neither Trident nor Rocket 3 came close to matching the CB750's impact.

TRIUMPH T150 TRIDENT (1969)

Engine	Aircooled 6-valve OHV pushrod transverse triple
Capacity	740cc (67 x 70mm)
Power	58bhp @ 7250rpm
Weight	213kg (468lb) dry
Top speed	125mph (201kph)

Triples were successful on the race circuit though, in particular "Slippery Sam", the Trident that won consecutive Production TTs between 1971 and 1975. Some of the best results came in America, where Gary Nixon had been AMA Grand National champion on Triumph twins in 1967 and 1968. The road-race triples used frames made by Rob North, with blue-and-white fairings for Triumph, and red-and-white for BSA. At Daytona in 1971, the triples took the first three places, Dick Mann winning on a BSA ahead of Triumph's Gene Romero, the reigning Grand National champion. Shortly afterwards, the triples were outpaced by Yamaha's two-strokes.

The most distinctive version of the triple was the Triumph X-75 Hurricane, a special built in limited numbers from 1972. The Hurricane was commissioned by Triumph's American distributor and designed by fairing and luggage specialist Craig Vetter. It combined a lower-geared version of the standard 740cc engine with longer front forks, a stylish tank/seat unit and a bold new three-silencer exhaust system, and was a predecessor of the modern Japanese factory customs.

In 1975, the basic triple was restyled and overhauled to produce the T160 Trident, which featured its engine angled forward in a new and improved frame. Numerous other modifications included an electric starter, rear disc brake and left-foot gearchange. Handsome styling, smooth power and excellent handling made the new Trident arguably the best British roadster so far, but it was not enough to save struggling Triumph, and production was short-lived.

■ TOP *The T160 Trident introduced in 1975 was both fast and stylish, but came too late to save Triumph.*

■ ABOVE LEFT *Triumph's works triples took riders including Paul Smart to many wins in the 1970s.*

■ ABOVE RIGHT *Meriden development rider and racer Percy Tait raced triples including the famous "Slippery Sam".*

■ LEFT *The lean looks of the X-75 Hurricane gained the American-designed factory special many admirers.*

TRIUMPH

■ TRIUMPH SPEED TRIPLE

The British motorcycle industry's decline seemed almost complete in 1983, when Triumph finally went into liquidation. But the name was bought by building multi-millionaire John Bloor, who spent the next eight years secretly developing a range of modern bikes in a purpose-built factory at Hinckley, near the old Meriden site. In 1991 Triumph released a range of six roadsters, powered by watercooled, DOHC three- and four-cylinder engines. Their unique modular design employed many identical components, reducing cost. Ironically, a series of modular designs

TRIUMPH SPEED TRIPLE (1994)

Engine	Watercooled 12-valve DOHC transverse triple
Capacity	885cc (76 x 65mm)
Power	97bhp @ 9000rpm
Weight	209kg (460lb) dry
Top speed	130mph (209kph)

produced by BSA-Triumph's engineers in 1973 had not been adopted.

Base model was the unfaired Trident, which had a 749 or 885cc three-cylinder engine. The larger unit produced 98bhp with plenty of mid-range torque, giving lively acceleration towards a top speed of 130mph (209kph). Like the other bikes the Trident had a large-diameter steel spine frame, with Japanese suspension and brakes. Top of the range

■ OPPOSITE TOP *The 1991 model Daytona 1000 sportster (left) and Trophy 1200 shared many parts.*

■ OPPOSITE BOTTOM *The popular Speed Triple of 1994 combined a three-cylinder engine with aggressive, naked styling.*

■ LEFT *Designed largely for the American market, the Thunderbird retro-bike was a hit worldwide in 1995.*

■ FAR LEFT *The basic Triumph model has been the unfaired Trident triple.*

■ BELOW LEFT *The Daytona 1200 gave 146bhp performance in 1993.*

was the 1200 Trophy, whose 123bhp four-cylinder engine was effectively the triple with an extra pot. Smooth, well built and capable of over 150mph (241kph), the Trophy was a match for the best Japanese sports tourers.

Triumph was rapidly successful in Britain. Exports also took off, after a slow start in the important German market. Triumph soon learnt to concentrate on its traditional triples, and in 1994 produced its most inspired model yet. The Speed Triple retained the original 885cc engine and spine frame, gaining upmarket cycle parts including multi-adjustable suspension, bigger brakes and fat radial tyres. The Speed Triple was quick, responsive and agile; and its name, lean styling and low, clip-on handlebars brought to mind the 1960s' days of

burn-ups and twin-cylinder Triumphs.

Nostalgia played an even greater part in the model that Triumph developed to spearhead its delayed return to America in 1995. The Thunderbird incorporated traditional styling features such as a rounded fuel tank with mouth-organ badges, and peashooter silencers. Exaggerated cooling fins gave a new look to the 885cc triple engine, which was detuned to a modest 69bhp. Other features, including raised bars, wire wheels and a lower seat, also moved away from the modular concept.

The T-bird's style and smooth, torquey engine made it a hit. With the expanding Hinckley factory's annual production due to exceed 10,000 for the first time, John Bloor's huge investment seemed to be paying off.

OTHER MAKES

■ URAL

From a big factory in the Ural mountains, the firm of the same name has long produced 650cc flat-twins based on BMW designs of the early 1940s. Inevitably crude by modern standards, most of the 250,000 bikes built annually were sold in the former Soviet Union. British importer Neval produced custom versions including the Soviet Knight, which combined the original 32bhp pushrod motor and simple

steel-framed chassis with high handlebars, running lights and added chrome. Handling was heavy and sophistication lacking, but the Soviet Knight was cheap and cruised smoothly at 60mph (96kph) with a certain old-fashioned charm.

■ RIGHT *High bars and added chrome gave the Soviet Knight a touch of Harley-style glamour, without the expense.*

VELOCETTE

■ BELOW *The sporty Clubman Venom of the early 1960s(left) was uprated to produce the Thruxton in 1965.*

■ BOTTOM *Thruxton features included tuned motor, uprated front brake, silver paint finish and humped seat.*

■ VELOCETTE VENOM THRUXTON

From the 1930s until its demise in 1971, Velocette was best known for its large-capacity four-stroke singles, most of them with traditional black-and-gold finish and a distinctive fishtail silencer. The firm was founded in 1904 by German-born Johannes Gütgemann, who later changed his name to John

VELOCETTE VENOM THRUXTON (1965)

Engine	Aircooled 2-valve OHV pushrod single
Capacity	499cc (86 x 86mm)
Power	40bhp @ 6200rpm
Weight	177kg (390lb) dry
Top speed	105mph (168kph)

Goodman, and was later run by his sons and grandson. Initially called Veloce Ltd, the company began by producing four-strokes. The first two-stroke, built in 1913, was called Velocette, after which the name was used for all of their subsequent models.

Velocette's racing involvement boosted development and prestige, although the expense was considerable. The Birmingham firm's first great bike was the overhead-cam 350cc single, designed by Percy Goodman, which won the 1926 Junior TT. Velocette's

■ BELOW LEFT
The 350cc MAC of the mid-1930s was a hugely successful machine.

■ BELOW RIGHT
Stanley Woods powers his Velo to Junior TT victory in 1939.

■ BOTTOM RIGHT
Neglecting singles to build the LE, pictured in Mk.2 form from 1955, proved disastrous for Velocette.

■ LEFT *The rapid 500cc parallel twin Roarer of 1939 was halted by the War and subsequent ban on supercharging.*

production version, the KTT, was the ultimate privateer racebike throughout the 1930s. The single was also popular in supersports form as the KSS, although it was sales of humbler pushrod singles such as the 350cc MAC and 500cc MSS that kept Velocette profitable.

After the Second World War, Velocette's racing success continued, notably with 350cc world championships for Freddie Frith and Bob Foster in 1949 and 1950. Best known roadsters were the 500cc Venom and 350cc Viper singles, which from 1960 were available in Clubmans trim with tuned engines and stiffer suspension. Fastest of all was the Venom Thruxton, released in 1965. Its tuned engine put out 40bhp and the chassis specification included alloy rims and a powerful twin-leading-shoe front brake. Typically hard to start, and rough at low speeds, the Thruxton – named after the Hampshire track used for long-distance production races – was a rapid street racer that could cruise at a respectable 90mph (145kph).

Velocette was also keen to produce less sporty bikes, and by 1949 almost all the singles had been dropped to make way for the revolutionary LE. This strange looking bike had legshields, a pressed-steel frame and a watercooled, flat-twin sidevalve engine, initially of 150cc. Although well built and reliable, the LE was also expensive. Even when uprated with a 192cc engine in 1951 the LE was popular only with the police, earning it the nickname "Noddy bike". The later Viceroy, a large 250cc scooter, proved even more disastrous, and Velocette went into liquidation in 1971.

OTHER MAKES

■ VAN VEEN
Henk van Veen was the Dutch importer of German Kreidlers. He took over the firm's race effort and led the Van Veen Kreidlers to a string of 50cc world championships in the 1970s. An even more ambitious project was the Van Veen OCR1000, a luxurious rotary-engined superbike. Although fast and smooth, the OCR was more remarkable for being the world's most expensive roadster in the late 1970s, and production was perhaps understandably short-lived.

■ VICTORIA
Like BMW, fellow German firm Victoria built flat-twins in the 1920s. Best known model was the V35 Bergmeister of the 1950s, a 350cc V-twin whose early vibration problems required lengthy development. Later bikes included the revolutionary 197cc Swing of 1956, which featured push-button gearchanging. In 1958 Victoria joined DKW and Express to form the Zweirad Union, but sales were poor and production came to an end in 1966.

■ ABOVE *The stylish and powerful Dutch-built Van Veen OCR1000 rotary was one of the most exotic Superbikes of the 1970s, but its inevitably high price limited sales.*

■ BELOW *Vincent's scroll logo, normally on a black background, adorned arguably the finest bikes of the 1950s.*

■ MIDDLE *The Black Shadow's 998cc V-twin engine featured tuned and polished internals plus black enamel finish.*

■ BOTTOM *Vincent's Series C Rapide combined thunderous performance with excellent handling and braking.*

VINCENT

■ VINCENT RAPIDE SERIES C

Fast, rugged and comfortable, Vincent's big V-twins were the ultimate high performance roadsters of their day. The firm was founded in 1928 by visionary engineer Philip Vincent, who as a schoolboy had designed the cantilever rear suspension system that all his bikes would use. Backed by his father, Vincent bought the defunct company HRD in an attempt to overcome market resistance to his first bikes, which used JAP single engines.

Vincent and Australian designer Phil Irving produced the Stevenage firm's first engine, a high camshaft 500cc single, in 1934. The resultant Meteor tourer and Comet sports singles were a success, the latter capable of an impressive 90mph (145kph). In 1936 Irving combined two Comet cylinders at 47 degrees to produce a 998cc, 45bhp V-twin. The Series A Rapide's 110mph (177kph) top speed

VINCENT RAPIDE SERIES C (1949)	
Engine	Aircooled 4-valve pushrod 50-degree V-twin
Capacity	998cc (84 x 90mm)
Power	45bhp @ 5200rpm
Weight	208kg (458lb) dry
Top speed	110mph (177kph)

made it the fastest production vehicle on the road, but the power led to transmission problems, and external oil lines led to the bike being nicknamed "the plumber's nightmare".

After the Second World War, Vincent introduced the Series B Rapide. This featured a redesigned 50-degree, unit-construction V-twin engine that was an integral part of the chassis, taking the place of the previous tubular frame. As

■ RIGHT *The Series A Rapide's 110mph (177kph) top speed made it the world's fastest roadster in the late 1930s.*

■ BELOW RIGHT *Only about 200 of the dramatic, fully enclosed Series D models were built, before production ended in 1955.*

OTHER MAKES

■ **WANDERER**

German firm Wanderer was founded in 1902 and built numerous singles and twins, some of which were used by the Germans in the First World War. Janecek of Prague built the Wanderer under licence, and in 1929 became the sole manufacturer as Janecek-Wanderer, later shortening the name to Jawa.

■ ABOVE *Wanderer produced this attractive little belt-drive V-twin, rated at 3.25bhp, in 1911.*

■ **WASP**

Chassis specialist Wasp began building off-road competition frames in 1968. The Wiltshire, England, firm's successful involvement in sidecar motocross led to production of its own 1000cc parallel twin engine in the early 1980s.

■ **WERNER**

The Russian-born, Paris-based Werner brothers, Michel and Eugene, were among motorcycling's greatest pioneers. Their first 217cc single, produced from 1898 onwards, was light and practical, and sold well. But the Werners are chiefly remembered for the innovative 1901-model New Werner whose layout, with the engine set low in a diamond-style bicycle frame, greatly improved handling and set the pattern for years to come.

well as reaching an effortless 100mph (160kph) at just 4600rpm, the mighty Rapide handled well and braked hard, thanks to twin drums on each wheel. In 1949 Vincent introduced the Series C Rapide, with Girdraulic forks replacing the previous Brampton girders.

The ultimate V-twin was the Black Shadow, introduced a year earlier, which was powered by a tuned, 55bhp black-finished engine. Top speed was a remarkable 120mph (193kph) plus, recorded on a speedometer calibrated to 150mph (241kph). That speed was achieved in the same year at Bonneville when Rollie Free, riding a tuned V-twin, stripped to swimming trunks and shoes to set a world record for unsupercharged bikes at 150.313mph (241.898kph). Other legendary Vincents were Gunga Din, Nero and the supercharged Super Nero, on which George Brown set speed records and won many races.

In 1955 Vincent introduced the Series D models, the Black Knight and tuned Black Prince. Despite Vincent's traditional high prices, the motorcycles were by then being sold at a loss, and production ceased at the end of the year. Hopes that the name would be revived came 40 years later, when American Bernard Li revealed plans for a traditionally styled but modern 1500cc V-twin roadster to be called the Vincent Black Eagle.

■ ABOVE *Rollie Free stripped to just a pair of bathing trunks to top 150mph (241kph) at Bonneville in 1948.*

■ ABOVE *The less sporty of Vincent's early 500cc singles was the Meteor, seen here in 1938 form.*

YAMAHA

■ YAMAHA 350cc YR5

Torakusu Yamaha trained as a clock-maker before, in 1897, founding Nippon Gakki, which grew into one of the world's largest musical instrument manufacturers. In 1955, Nippon Gakki established the Yamaha company to build motorbikes, using machinery that had made aircraft propellers in the Second World War. The first bike was a 125cc two-stroke single called the YA-1 or Red Dragonfly, based on a German DKW. The twin-cylinder YD-1 followed in 1957 and Yamaha began establishing a reputation for quick, light and reliable two-strokes, many of which featured the company's tuning fork logo on the tank.

■ ABOVE LEFT *Good handling combined with brisk acceleration and competitive price to ensure the YR5's success.*

■ MIDDLE LEFT *Victory in the 1955 Asama road race helped the YA-1's reputation.*

■ BELOW *The shape of the YR5, and the RD350, was echoed in many smaller Yamahas.*

■ LEFT *Phil Read heads for victory in the 250cc TT in 1971, the year he won his fourth world title for Yamaha.*

■ RIGHT *Future Grand Prix star Niall Mackenzie heads a typically frenzied battle in a RD350 Pro-Am race in 1983.*

YAMAHA 350cc YR5 (1970)

Engine	Aircooled reed-valve two-stroke parallel twin
Capacity	347cc (64 x 54mm)
Power	36bhp @ 7000rpm
Weight	150kg (330lb) wet
Top speed	95mph (152kph)

■ ABOVE *Yamaha's first four-stroke roadster, the XS-1 of 1969, copied British bikes with its 650cc parallel twin engine.*

In the 1960s, Yamaha's successful series of 250cc YDS models led to the first 350cc twin, the YR1. In 1970, the firm released the neatly styled YR5, its aircooled parallel twin engine producing a maximum of 36bhp, which was enough to send the lightweight Yamaha screaming to 95mph (152kph). Handling and braking were good, reliability was excellent, price was competitive and the YR5 became hugely popular. Notable successors included the six-speed RD350 of 1974; the angular, 100mph (160kph) RD400 of 1976; the watercooled, single-shock RD350LC of 1981; and the legendary 1983 model YPVS or Power Valve, whose exhaust power valve improved mid-range performance and helped produce a claimed 53bhp, over 50 per cent up on the YR5's output. The fully-faired RD350LC F2 that followed was still being built, in Brazil, in the mid-1990s.

Yamaha's first period of Grand Prix success came in the 1960s, in the smaller classes. Phil Read won the 250cc title in 1964 on the parallel twin RD56 – the first time it had been won by a two-stroke – and retained it the following season. For 1967, Yamaha built a 35bhp, 16,000rpm V-four on which Bill Ivy won that year's 125cc title. Following Honda's retirement from racing, Yamaha intended to share the 1968 championships between teammates Read and Ivy. But Read, with the 125cc crown safe, controversially refused to play that game and went on to take the 250cc title too.

Yamaha's first four-stroke roadster was the 650cc XS-1 of 1969, a British-style parallel twin that was capable of 105mph (168kph). In America the twin was competitively priced and was a success, particularly when updated to produce a series of XS650 models. The last of these, the US-market Heritage Special cruiser, brought the XS into the early 1980s, by which time production had soared well into six figures.

■ RIGHT *The fast and popular RD350LC Power Valve was available with or without a fairing in the late 1980s.*

YAMAHA

■ YAMAHA FZR1000

The bike that brought Yamaha to the forefront of superbike design was the four-cylinder FZR1000, which many riders regarded as the best Japanese sportster in the years following its launch in 1987. Its powerplant was a watercooled, 989cc engine whose angled-forward cylinder layout and DOHC, 20-valve cylinder head format had been introduced on the FZ750 two years earlier. The FZR's peak output of 125bhp matched that of Suzuki's GSX-R1100, class leader at the time.

Yamaha's Genesis factory racebike provided inspiration for the FZR's chassis, which centred on a rigid aluminium twin-spar Deltabox frame. Cycle parts included stout 41mm forks, a 17-inch front wheel and low-profile radial tyres. The motor was more than impressive, pulling smoothly from low revs until the FZR was hurtling towards its top speed of 160mph (257kph), with its rider crouching behind an efficient twin-headlamp fairing. Handling and braking were also excellent, and the Yamaha rapidly became hugely popular.

Numerous updates in subsequent years succeeded in retaining the FZR's cutting edge – notably in 1989 when Yamaha enlarged the motor to 1002cc and added an electronically operated exhaust valve whose acronym led to the bike being universally known as the EXUP. The system added useful mid-range performance; peak power was also increased, to 140bhp. A comprehensively revamped chassis provided improved handling to match, making the EXUP the pick of the Japanese Superbikes. Two years later the package was further improved with the FZR1000RU, featuring sharper styling and upside-down front forks.

In marked contrast to the light and agile FZR1000, Yamaha's first big four, the 1978 model XS1100, was a Japanese Superbike of the old school – a large, powerful, aircooled engine in a heavy chassis that was barely capable of keeping it under control. The 1101cc twin-cam motor produced a maximum of 95bhp and was particularly memorable for its huge reserves of mid-range

YAMAHA FZR1000RU (1991)

Engine	Watercooled 20-valve DOHC transverse four
Capacity	1002cc (75.5 x 56mm)
Power	140bhp @ 10,000rpm
Weight	209kg (461lb) dry
Top speed	168mph (269kph)

■ BELOW *By the early 1990s the FZR1000 had been overtaken by faster sportsbikes, but still remained a fine machine.*

■ LEFT *The FZR1000's torquey, 140bhp engine meant that wheelies were only a twist of the throttle away.*

■ RIGHT *The powerful and fine-handling FZ750 of 1985 did not attract the sales that it deserved.*

■ RIGHT *Few rival sports-tourers have approached the FJ1200's blend of speed and long-distance comfort.*

torque, which gave effortless acceleration to a top speed of 135mph (217kph). The XS was also smooth, comfortable and well-equipped. But the shaft-drive Yamaha's bulk and 270kg (595lb) of weight made for ponderous handling and instability at high speed, which severely limited its appeal.

Although Yamaha's FJ1100 was billed as a pure sportsbike when it was launched in 1984, the aircooled four quickly found its niche as a smooth, comfortable and effortlessly fast sports-tourer. It looked good, handled well, had a protective fairing and a 150mph (241kph) top speed, and most of all its broad powerband gave instant acceler-ation from almost any engine speed. That was even truer of the FJ1200, created in 1986 by enlarging the 16-valve engine to 1188cc. In the 1990s Yamaha intro-duced further refinements, including a rubber-mounted engine and anti-lock brakes, that kept the FJ popular after over ten years in production.

YAMAHA

■ YAMAHA YZR500

Yamaha's YZR has been the dominant 500cc Grand Prix bike of the modern era, winning six world championships between 1984 and 1993, and also providing the basis for the ROC and Harris-framed privateer V-fours of recent seasons. The Japanese factory's experience with 500cc V-fours began with Kenny Roberts' disc-valve OW61

YAMAHA YZR500 (1991)

Engine	Watercooled 80-degree V-four crankcase reed-valve two-stroke
Capacity	498cc (56 x 50.6mm)
Power	165bhp @ 12,500rpm
Weight	130kg (286lb) dry
Top speed	190mph (304kph)

■ ABOVE *Eddie Lawson won the 1986 Dutch TT on the way to the second of his three world titles on the YZR500.*

■ LEFT *Six world titles in the decade following its introduction emphasized the YZR500's impact on Grand Prix racing.*

■ LEFT *Wayne Rainey (17) took over from Eddie Lawson (3) to win a hat-trick of titles for Yamaha.*

OTHER MAKES

■ ZENITH

A leading marque in the early years of the century, Zenith was best known for the popular Gradua with its adjustable gearing, operated by a long, so-called coffee grinder hand lever. Zenith built Villiers and JAP-engined singles in the 1930s, but production effectively ended at the start of the Second World War.

■ ZÜNDAPP

One of the major German firms for many years, Zündapp was founded in 1917 initially to make gun parts. Successful bikes included numerous flat-twins such as the KS750, much used by German troops in the Second World War, and the sporty 1951 model KS601, known as the Green Elephant. Zündapp thrived in the 1960s and 1970s, producing successful off-road competition bikes and two-stroke roadsters. But sales fell dramatically in the early 1980s. Stefan Dörflinger won the 80cc world title for Zündapp in 1984, but the firm went into liquidation the following year.

of 1982. The YZR, with its crankcase reed-valve induction system, was introduced as the OW81 model in 1984. Its engine used twin crankshafts geared together, the layout actually more accurately resembling a W4. This format has also been adopted by Suzuki and Cagiva, leaving only Honda's NSR as a true V-four.

The YZR's output has risen gradually over the years, to a figure of over 180bhp from the recent big bang unit. Chassis layout has remained typical of a Grand Prix 500, based around a thick twin-spar aluminium frame, with suspension generally provided by Öhlins, the Swedish specialist firm owned by Yamaha. In many seasons the YZR has not been the fastest bike in a straight line, but it has been tractable, reliable and a good all-rounder, capable of winning at any circuit, especially at the hands of strars like Californians Eddie Lawson and Wayne Rainey, both of whom rode it to three world championships.

Arguably the greatest racebikes of the 1970s were Yamaha's TZs, from the TZ250 twin to the TZ750 four. After winning its first race in 700cc form in 1974, the four dominated Formula 750 racing for the rest of the decade. Powerful and fast yet impressively reliable, the TZ750 won four F750 titles and was still capable of taking Graeme Crosby to Daytona victory in 1982. Agostini won Yamaha's first 500cc world championship on a straight four in 1975, ending MV's four-stroke domination. Most successful of all was Kenny Roberts, who rode the four to a hat-trick of titles between 1978 and 1980.

■ ABOVE *Frenchman Christian Sarron won the 250cc world championship on Yamaha's TZ twin in 1984..*

■ RIGHT AND INSET RIGHT *Kenny Roberts won world titles with Yamaha as a rider and, more recently, as a manager.*

INDEX